Critical Human Geography

'Critical Human Geography' is an international series which provides a critical examination and extension of the concepts and
consequences of work in human geography and the allied social
sciences and humanities. The volumes are written by scholars
currently engaged in substantive research, so that, wherever possible,
the discussions are empirically grounded as well as theoretically
informed. Existing studies and the traditions from which they derive
are carefully described and located in their historically specific
context, but the series at the same time introduces and explores new
ideas and insights from the human sciences as a whole. The series is
thus not intended as a collection of synthetic reviews, but rather as a
cluster of considered arguments which are accessible enough to
engage geographers at all levels in the development of geography.
The series therefore reflects the continuing methodological and
philosophical diversity of the subject, and its books are united only by
their common commitment to the prosecution of a genuinely human
geography.

Department of Geography   MARK BILLINGE
University of Cambridge   DEREK GREGORY
England   RON MARTIN

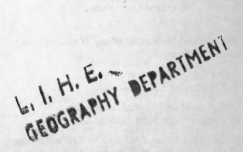

Critical Human Geography

PUBLISHED

Recollections of a Revolution: Geography as Spatial Science
Mark Billinge, Derek Gregory and Ron Martin (*editors*)

The Arena of Capital
Michael Dunford and Diane Perrons

Regional Transformation and Industrial Revolution:
A Geography of the Yorkshire Woollen Industry
Derek Gregory

Geography and the State: An Essay in Political Geography
R. J. Johnston

Spatial Divisions of Labour: Social Structures and
the Geography of Production
Doreen Massey

Conceptions of Space in Social Thought: A Geographic
Perspective
Robert David Sack
The Urban Arena: Capital, State and Community
in Contemporary Britain
John R. Short

FORTHCOMING

A Cultural Geography of Industrialisation in Britain
Mark Billinge

Development Theory: A Critique of Essentialist Approaches
Stuart Corbridge and Steve Jones

Between Feudalism and Capitalism
Robert Dodgshon

Regions and the Philosophy of the Human Sciences
Nicholas Entrikin

Strategies for Geographical Enquiry
Derek Gregory and Ron Martin

Social Relations and Spatial Structures
Derek Gregory and John Urry (*editors*)

De-Industrialisation and the British Space Economy
Ron Martin and Bob Rowthorn (*editors*)

The Urban Arena

Capital, State and Community in Contemporary Britain

John R. Short

MACMILLAN

First published 1984 by
Higher and Further Education Division
MACMILLAN PUBLISHERS LTD
London and Basingstoke
Companies and representatives
throughout the world

Printed in Hong Kong

British Library Cataloguing in Publication Data
Short, John R.
The urban arena: capital, state and community
in contemporary Britain.
1. Great Britain—Economic policy—1945.
I. Title
330.941′0858   HC256.6
ISBN 0-333-36139-3
ISBN 0-333-36140-7 Pbk

For Adrienne

Contents

Acknowledgements

The writing of this book would not have been possible without the supportive atmosphere provided by my departmental colleagues at the University of Reading. I am particularly indebted to the staff of the drawing office for the production of the diagrams and to Chris Holland for transferring my Scottish vowels, excitable lilt and swallowed words on to the printed page. She is a marvellous typist.

I owe a special debt to Derek Gregory, who readily accepted a few jottings as proof of a manuscript and gave up the 'joys' of fatherhood for the 'delights' of editing a wild and woolly manuscript: he made many valuable suggestions.

JOHN R. SHORT

The author and publishers wish to thank the following who have kindly given permission for the use of copyright material: Chetwynd Haddons Ltd for the advertisement 'Deep in the Shropshire Countryside we've set up a completely New State' on behalf of the Telford Development Corporation; Clydebank Task Force, Scottish Development Agency, for two advertisements 'A Deal as Great as our Reputation' and 'Scotland's Enterprise Zone. Several jumps ahead'; The Controller of Her Majesty's Stationery Office for a figure from the Wilson Report, and two figures from the Economic Progress Report Nos 135 and 198; The Economist Newspaper Ltd for three charts from *The Economist*; Industrial Development Board for Northern Ireland for their advertisement 'New Technology? Our Northern Ireland workers take it in their stride'; The Institute of British Geographers for two figures from *Area*; Redditch Development Corporation for their advertisement 'There are important losses to be gained by moving to Redditch'; Rex Stewart, Mitchell Frise Ltd for the advertisement 'New Company? New Factory?' on behalf of the Borough of Newport; Warrington Runcorn Development Corporation for their advertisement 'The right move for . . .'.

1
Introduction

The urban

The concern with urban matters has long been a feature of social commentary in Britain. In the nineteenth century the scale and pace of urbanisation was tremendous. Bustling towns seemed to grow over green fields and quite market towns were transformed into major cities. In the course of only a few Victorian decades the predominantly agricultural landscape was studded with coke-towns and a predominantly rural population became city dwellers. For some, the urban transformation was something to be feared as the city became a symbol of the breakdown in traditional social order. The fear of social unrest, the problems of drunkenness, vice and disease in the poor city areas were all seen as symptoms of a moral and social collapse. For others, the city became a kind of early social science laboratory in which the facts of social existence were noted and recorded. While the Livingstones were in Africa, the Booths and Mayhews were exploring darkest London. For yet others the city became the symbol of a new order. Urban industrial life according to Marx and Engels saved people from rural idiocy and gave workers an indication and experience of collective struggle; the city was the womb of a new, better society.

As the twentieth century progressed the novelty of the urban faded. Urban living and working became the norm. The specificity of the urban was only raised to a significant level in popular academic debates in the 1960s and 1970s. The long, post-war economic boom was coming to an end and the general layer of affluence which overlaid private experience and popular culture was stripped off to reveal the old fracture lines of class and the new ones of race and gender. Pockets of poverty were being mapped and victims of multiple deprivation were being recorded in inner city locations. Again, the

1

fear and reality of social unrest signalled a new concern with the urban experience.

This book is part of that long British tradition of urban concern. But it differs from most of its predecessors by the exact focus of its interest. I am less concerned with pointing to the specificity of the urban: we have come too far down the road to identify any specific urban facet independent from the nature of the wider society. I am rather more concerned with identifying the urban as a context for social processes. All social actions take place in space and our lived experience is not of grand sociological categories but of small-scale places. This is a truism which would scarcely need repeating were it not for the neglect of space in most social theories. In too many cases the ability to analyse social actions is made deficient by the inability to see the interplay between space and society, place and people, social processes and spatial structure. There is a need to reinsert a consideration of the spatial context, a need for an explicit environmental vocabulary in our considerations of society. In this book I will take just one component of our environmental context, the urban. The term 'urban' is used interchangeably with 'local' since most of the British population live in towns and cities. It is possible to consider other environmental contexts, the nation-state, the neighbourhood, the countryside, etc. Each has its own set of processes, constellations of interest and conflicts. Together they make up the reality of our lives. It is legitimate to demarcate an urban component because distinct interests are articulated in this environment. Firms make investment decisions on international, national and *urban* scales, governments operate on the national and *urban* scale, households as users of public services, workers and residents live in particular *urban* places.

It is the aim of this book to examine these interests and to note their interaction. I will limit my remarks to the contemporary period. Although the urban experience in other advanced capitalist countries will be considered, the focus is on Britain. It is impossible to compare the rich and varied experience in a range of countries in an exposition of this kind without degenerating into a breathless survey insensitive to importance differences. But only the focus is parochial, the wider goal is to add to our knowledge of capitalist societies.

The arena

Three of the main interests (or players if you want to carry the analogy further) in the urban arena are *capital*, the *community* and the *state*. The pursuit of their respective interests involves sources of tension, conflict, routine interaction and irregular contact all of which constitute the very warp and weft of contemporary urban affairs. The broad labels used cover a variety of interests. Under the umbrella term of 'capital', for example, there is industrial capital, finance capital and property capital, each differing in aims, modes of operation and urban impact and there is a whole gamut of community groups with varying degrees of power and influence. For the moment however the terms will be defined in shorthand notation only. They will be unpacked for more careful analysis in later chapters.

Capital: places and profits

The term 'capital' is often used in the standard economic literature to refer to real assets (factories, machinery, etc.) and financial assets (stocks, securities, etc.); hence the term 'capital expenditure' to refer to spending on such assets. But this definition only captures the physical expression of capital. Above all, capital is a social relationship. I will use the term to refer to the power of command over labour and its products in order to create wealth. The production and distribution of wealth depends upon the struggle between capital and labour. Their relationship is not of symbiotic antagonism. When labour is strong, for example, it can influence the labour process in order to achieve better working conditions and higher wages. Labour can also seek to achieve better living conditions. Until fairly recently it has been a feature of capital–labour relations in Britain for the conflict to be contained within the factory gates: labour's main concern has been with the point of production rather than with areas of reproduction. But this has been changing. The rise of community action and its fusion with the labour movement in certain places has been a striking facet of political affairs. An important point of contact has been the alliance over job losses and community disruption in the wake of economic restructuring and commercial developments.

Capital is concerned with making profit. For capital the city is a place in which to make money. As we shall see, this often involves a conflict with the community, the state and parts of organised labour. While labour and community tend to be tied to particular areas, certain fractions of capital are much more mobile. The disparity between this mobility of capital and relative immobility of labour often expresses itself in a conflict over patterns of capital investment and disinvestment in particular places. The interests of labour tend to be rooted in particular places. Capital in contrast is foot-loose. The story is not one of continual conflict, of course, because certain fractions of capital are fixed in space, and where place devaluation is occurring there is the basis for regional and city alliances between capital and labour. However, the increasing concentration and internationalisation of capital signals the decline of specifically local capitals. Capital is concerned with profit and thus with places as generators of wealth. The concern with other aspects of places rarely extends beyond the factory gates or the office doorway. When it does, the concern is with reducing costs and directing government expenditure to the needs of capital.

The community: places as living space

I will use the term 'community' to refer to households as residents of particular places. Members of the community are payers of local rates and taxes, users of local services, voters and workers. Community concerns are local concerns with urban places as workplaces, residencies and living areas. The welfare of individuals is a product of their position in the socio-economic hierarchy and a function of their location in space. Much attention has been lavished on the former. Less attention has been focused on the latter. In this book I will seek to correct the imbalance.

Locational politics is an important element in contemporary Britain. In the constantly changing urban areas residents seek to maximise the provision of public 'goods' (e.g. parks) and benefit from positive externalities while deflecting public 'bads' and negative externalities. An increasingly important feature in recent years have been community concerns with jobs and employment opportunities. But community cleavages overlap, exacerbate and sometimes contradict class divisions, so that it is legitimate to separate out community concerns from the concerns of labour. Issues of reproduction do not always neatly mesh with divisions produced at the point of production.

The state: scene of action

I will use the term 'state' to refer to both the government of elected representatives and the various state apparatuses of judiciary, police, civil service, etc. In later chapters I will seek to show the influence of the main state apparatus. For the moment I will limit my remarks to the government. At both the local and national level, elected representatives are meant to represent community concerns. Both MPs and councillors are elected on a community basis. But reflected through the lens of party politics these community concerns are also rationalised with respect to sectoral interests. Although the link between trade unions and the Labour party, and capital and the Conservative party fails to note the subtle nuances involved, it does capture the broad outline of the relationships. In Britain, as in most advanced capitalist societies, the government is the terrain of struggle between different interests, primarily capital and labour. These interests refracted through political representation are broadly reflected in the direction of policy and funding. Two broad types of domestic policy can be identified:

1. The concern with maintaining profit levels. O'Connor (1973) has termed this the *accumulation function* of government. It involves such things as public expenditure on roads, reductions in corporation tax, weakening the power of unions, etc.
2. Meeting popular demands. The mass of people, through the ballot box, can achieve some measure of the welfare

provision; for example, rights to education, social insurance and public health schemes, etc. O'Connor has termed this the legitimation function but since this term seems to imply that provision of such facilities is always merely a successful bribe, an incorporation of popular demands, I will use the term *welfare function.*

In practice there is not such a neat division, and the crude dichotomy fails to capture the way individual public policies are stamped with conflict. Moreover, these policies are frequently justified by appeals to ideologies which transcend this simple division. Accumulation expenditure is often justified on the grounds of national interest, for example, while welfare expenditure is criticized as a drain on the resources of the country. From other, centrist perspectives, in contrast, welfare expenditure is often justified as necessary for capital accumulation through the promise of social harmony and the inculcation of a willing workforce. In short, compromises are struck in thought just as bargains are struck in practice. Clearly, much public policy-making and public expenditure is guided by bureaucratic considerations and what we might call incrementalism, rather than being a direct result of policy changes in the wake of political changes. But as the political balance shifts so the level and direction of public spending changes. Particular items of expenditure cannot be simply associated either with capitals' requirements or the needs of labour. Public expenditure is part of the tension.

If we look at the two main types of expenditure in detail we can see that they represent the twin facets of places. Accumulation expenditure is concerned with places as work-places, as places of profit, while welfare expenditure is much more concerned with places as living spaces. The conflicts between capital and community and the concern with cities as 'profitopolis' as opposed to cities as places to live are expressed through the direction of policy and the destination of public expenditure. Overlying this tension is the division between central and local government. Government in Britain consists of central government as law-maker and main banker, and local government which represents local areas and carries out central government policies. Central government is concerned with places as political platforms while local government is much more closely associated with particular places, local concerns, with cities as living places. The conflict between central and local government, especially when sharpened by divisions between Labour-controlled city authorities and central Conservative governments, is thus the conflict between the accumulation and welfare functions of government, and reflects the tensions between the interests of capital and the needs of the community. Debates over public expenditure and central–local relations are the surface manifestation of the tensions between capital and community expressed through the language and practice of government.

In the rest of this book I will seek to elaborate these points. It is as well to consider the broad context and the specific conjuncture which have heightened the tensions. In the next chapter I will briefly review the broad trends of post-war Britain, not to provide a definitive survey but to present a context for the exposition which follows.

The approach

Authors have a duty to their readers to lay bare the assumptions which underlie their work. The substantive thesis of this book is that there is a tension in the relationships between capital and labour and between capital and community mediated through and reflected in the state. The term tension is used to refer to the differing, often competing interests. The attempted resolution of these conflicts is the very stuff of British politics.

The approach can best be illuminated by contrasting it with the extremes on either side. On the one hand there is the apologist view which sees a harmony of interest and a neutral state. On the other there is the crude Marxist view which concentrates on the capital–labour relation and sees in it an unreconcilable conflict driven by the state acting as a big stick (but sometimes a carrot) in the hands of capital. Compared to these theological systems which are immune from empirical verification, the approach offered here is one of cautious agnosticism. I believe that there is conflict between the agents identified because their interests differ. But within certain limits the relationship is a constantly changing one. While others have considered the limits – for example, Harvey (1982) – I want to look at the internal changes within these bounds, the nuances in what I have called the 'symbiotic antagonism'. My conception of the state is thus neither of a giant referee nor of a capitalist tool. It is rather the scene of struggle, the terrain of conflict, an arena within the arena of capital. The state has been used by labour and the community to achieve real gains which cannot be dismissed as sops. To concentrate on the harmony or the unreconcilable conflict is to relate the unfolding relationships to an already constructed theoretical edifice protected from the reality of social struggle. My concern is with the relationships and their unfolding, not with fitting them into an explanatory structure so tight it leaves little room for everchanging historical configurations.

The exposition is relatively straightfoward. In the next chapter I will consider the main developments in post-war Britain which have lead to the sharpening of conflict. In Chapter 3 the response of capital to the decline of the post-war boom is considered, in Chapter 4 the response of the state to economic decline is examined, while chapter 5 looks at the increasing role and form of community concerns.

This book carries on and extends work I have done elsewhere. In effect it is the second of three related works. The first, *An Introduction to Political Geography* (Short, 1982a), provides a world context for the position of Britain outlined in the present book. The third, *Land Housing and Conflict*, will extend the debates of the present book by looking at one particular region in Britain, Central Berkshire, noting in more detail the precise unfolding of relations between capital, the community and the state in an area of growth.

2
The Context

The boom: expansion and compromise

The post-war period up to the late 1960s saw the largest
expansion of economic growth the world has ever seen. The
period saw an expanding world economy based on the
reduction of tarriff barriers, the development of new technology, the existence of large pools of labour all underwritten
by a dollar currency. A self-perpetuating cycle of growth was
created. The main beneficiary was the United States which had
set up the system in order to break into world markets, but
other advanced capitalist countries also gained. In Britain the
endemic problems of declining productivity and poor economic performance were masked by this huge expansion of
world trade and increased demand.

For individuals this post-war boom meant rising incomes
and new job opportunities and effectively sealed the bargain
struck between capital and labour during the war and in the
immediate post-war years. The Second World War had proved
a radicalising experience in Britain and a powerful position had
been afforded to organised labour. The result was, as after the
First World War, a demand for a new social order and a
climate which encouraged new solutions to old problems. A
White Paper on full employment published in 1944 and the
Beveridge Report of 1945 signalled the main outlines of the
new order. The Keynes–Beveridge mix was one of full
employment and an extensive social welfare scheme. Jobs were
to be available for those able to work and those unable to do so
were to be given relatively high levels of benefits. These two
papers were only part of a flood of documents and legislation
produced in the later years of the war mapping out the course
of a new Britain. Others involved the creation of a strong
planning system and the commitment to educational provision. The demands for social change were crystallised in the

massive election victory of the Labour party in 1945. Many of the wartime proposals were put into effect by the 1945–51 Labour governments.

Post-war Britain saw an enlargement of the public sector, more state involvement in the running of the economy and much higher levels of public expenditure. Public expenditure rose to 45 per cent of GNP, whereas in the inter-war period it had only been around 25 per cent. Government expenditure was rising to similar levels in Western Europe and North America but in Britain a greater burden was placed on capital. Between 1938 and 1951 pre-tax shares of profits in national income rose from 12 to 14 per cent but post-tax fell from 9 to 5 per cent.

The compromise between capital and labour was ultimately predicated upon a booming world economy which meant full employment and rising incomes. The ability of the market to provide material goods, job security and a high social wage legitimised the social order and sanctioned the mixed economy.

Economic growth did have its costs. Fields were turned into factories, pollutants flowed into rivers and smoke belched into the skies. The costs of economic growth were paid in an environmental currency as pollution increased and scarce resources were used up. The so-called 'limits to growth' argument (Meadows *et al.*, 1972) pointed to the long-term dangers of continued levels of growth, and the rise of the environmental movement is perhaps one of the most important legacies of the period of sustained growth. Others have pointed to even less tangible costs. Seabrook (1982), for example, has pointed to the impoverishment of working-class ideology. As washing-machines and cars became the index of the 'good life' the older traditions of working-class culture were eroded. As boom turned into recession the effect was to leave the unemployed no cultural stock to fall back on: unemployment became an individual failure not a social concern, not an indictment of the system but merely an inability to buy consumer goods. Seabrook perhaps overstates the case, washing-machines, for example, have been a liberation for many working-class mothers) and he assumes too easy a co-option by the dominant ideology (cf. Abercrombie *et al.*, 1980).

More generally, it is too easy to draw a causal connection between the consumption of material goods and the erosion of older ideologies. Nevertheless, Seabrook is correct in pointing to the lack of an articulated and popular alternative conception of social life and individual expression to that portrayed in and through the capitalist system. Modern poverty is marked by an emotional bleakness as much as an inability to purchase consumer goods and the means of life.

The slump: decline and tensions

The world economy

The collapse of the boom was already becoming apparent by the mid to late 1960s and was decisively signalled by the 1973–4 recession. As the pools of labour were soaked up labour shortages appeared, and because of the consequent greater bargaining power of organised labour, higher wage claims were being made and met. The competition between capitals for the same labour also played a part in forcing up wage levels often above increases in productivity. It was not only labour costs which were rising. Raw material producers were also putting up their prices. From January 1974 the oil-producing countries quadrupled the price of oil. The effect was dramatic. Energy costs soared and there was a sudden abrupt shift in the balance of economic power. The oil producers became the *nouveaux riches* of the world economy. Other raw material producers also attempted to form cartels in a complex series of negotiations, and overall the net effect was to increase raw material costs to the industries of the capitalist world.

Firms found it difficult to pass on these cost increases through price increases because of foreign competition, and their room for manoeuvre was further constrained by labour resistance to productivity deals. As more net product was going to labour and raw material suppliers so profits fell. Figure 2.1 shows the general pattern. In the face of declining profits, investments fell: in effect an investment strike. In the early 1970s the then British Prime Minister, Edward Heath,

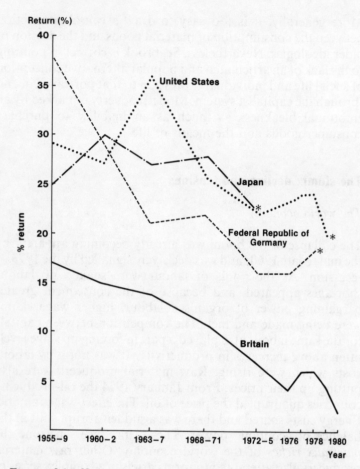

FIGURE 2.1   *Net rates of return on capital in manufacturing industry*

* Latest available figures.

SOURCE: Organisation for Economic Co-operation and Development.

told his audience at the Institute of Directors:

> When we came in we were told that there were not sufficient
> inducements to invest. So we provided the inducements.
> Then we were told people were scared of balance of

payments difficulties leading to stop–go. So we floated the
pound. Then we were told of fears of inflation: and now we
are dealing with that. And still you are not investing enough!

It was not profitable for capital to be invested in plant and
machinery if commodities could not be sold at a 'reasonable'
profit. For individual manufacturing companies feeling the
pinch the answer was to close down old plants, shed labour and
try to increase productivity. Within individual sectors the
weaker firms went bankrupt. Unemployment increased and
industry as a whole placed less orders. While individual firms
were responding rationally the net effect of their separate
responses was an overall decline in purchasing power. After
1974 there was a downward spiral of a decline in aggregate
demand leading to yet more unemployment. Inflation began to
increase as firms tried to increase profits by increasing prices,
workers sought to obtain wage increases to cover these costs
and the state increased the money supply in order to satisfy the
conflicting demands. By the mid to late 1970s the long boom
had ended. The term 'slumpflation' described the scene of
declining economic activity, increasing unemployment and
high inflation. As the 1970s turned into the 1980s recession was
turning into depression as unemployment continued to rise and
inflation was tempered but not tamed. The tension between
capital and labour, between profit and weflare which the boom
had managed to hide with the experience of private affluence
and public expenditure was being revealed anew.

The British experience

The tensions were particularly acute in Britain because of the
speed and extent of economic decline. In a broad historical
sweep Gamble (1981) has shown how the factors that made
Britain so successful in the nineteenth century have become the
reasons behind the decline in the twentieth. He cites three.
First, the British economy was firmly inserted into a world
order. Britain's nineteenth-century success lay in its powerful
navy and its strong position in a free market system. The
commitment to both the world role and the free market stance

continued long after the original reasons for them had evaporated. The result was a costly defence budget in the post-war period and an economy open to external shocks and foreign competition. 'Free trade' is the ideology of a successful economy, but for an uncompetitive one it borders on economic suicide. Second, there was the particular position of the state in British society. Throughout the seventeenth and eighteenth centuries the state's function was seen as the protection of private interests. The decline of the powers of the monarch saw in its stead the growth of a permissive state, one which gave latitude to market forces. In the nineteenth century this provided a boom to British commerce and trade. While other economies continued to be shackled by feudal chains, the British economy was free to grow and expand. By the middle of the twentieth century, however, such a non-interventionist state hampered development as political parties fought out issues on old dogmas. The permissive state which had been an advantage in the nineteenth century had become a dis-advantage by the twentieth. While other countries had reached a degree of internal compromise, the fabric of British politics was riven by disputes over the precise role of the state and the division between the public and private sectors. The state played a minimal and controversial role in regenerating the British economy. Finally, Gamble points to the power of the working class. This class through the organised labour move-ment and the Labour party could limit the power of capital. The power of the working class also influenced political disputes over the precise role of the state. In countries where the capitalist class is politically all-powerful then the role of the state is not a contentious issue; but in countries like Britain where there is a powerful and explicit working-class movement the role of the state becomes more contentious because the state can be used for major redistributional enterprises. The power of the working class in Britain is a vigorous force affecting the capital–labour relations and the extent and direction of state involvement.

In sum, the preconditions of economic growth and capital accumulation in the nineteenth century became the brakes on successful adaptation to the changed conditions of the twentieth. During the post-war boom the relative weakness of the British economy lay hidden, but as the boom turned into slump relative decline turned into absolute decline. Figure 2.2 shows the steady downward trend in Britain's share of world trade. The British experience compared unfavourably with that of her economic rivals. In the 1950s and 1960s Britain was locked in a vicious circle of slow growth compared to the benign spiral of other countries. In Japan and the Federal Republic of Germany, for example, the emphasis was on the

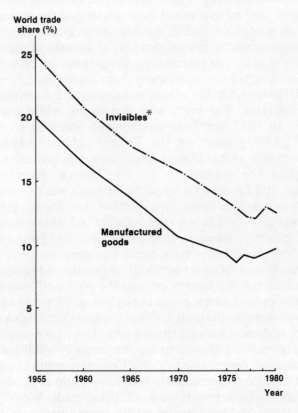

FIGURE 2.2 *Britain's share in world trade*

SOURCE: *The Economist.*

domestic economy and export performance. There was high
investment which, along with the introduction of efficient mass
production techniques, increased productivity. Prices of export
goods remained competitive and the domestic economy was
stimulated by increased wages. Growth bred growth. In Britain
by contrast sections of capital and most of the government
were less concerned with domestic production and commodity
exports. The interests of the City were with maintaining
exports of capital and securing the position of sterling. As
Brittan (1964) noted in his assessment of post-war economic
management under the Tories, domestic growth was sacrificed
for the sake of sterling. The belief in fixed exchange rates and
the role of sterling as a world currency limited the manoeuvrability of successive British governments. Domestic growth
was also sacrificed at crucial periods for the sake of maintaining a world role. The rearmament programme of 1950–2, for
example, diverted resources away from export industries and
delayed the introduction of new techniques and the winning of
export markets. The myth of a continuing world role still
persists. In 1982 the Tory government preferred to spend
almost £8,000 million on the Trident submarine-launched
nuclear missile rather than to invest in roads and railways.

Whereas the trajectories of the Federal Republic of
Germany and Japan were upwards, Britain's was downwards.
There was a vicious downward spiral of slow growth generat-
ing slower growth. The low profits meant lack of investment in
British industry, which in turn led to declining productivity.
While foreign factories were being equipped with the latest
machines British factories were still using outdated equipment.
All the comparative figures indicate the poor performance of
Britain in growth rates, productivity, share of world exports
and investment. In the early 1950s this was occurring as a result
of a lack of domestic competition as the old wartime cartels and
price agreements continued to create monopoly conditions and
there were still favourable ties with Commonwealth countries.
At that time there seemed little need to re-equip as goods were
still being sold and profits were still being made. World trade
was booming and even inefficient British industries could sell
their goods. Productivity increases were also limited by the role
of organised labour in limiting the application of labour-saving

devices: the introduction of new equipment which meant job losses was vigorously resisted. The conditions of full employment gave extra bargaining power to labour.

As the post-war boom began to tail off in the mid 1960s the sharp elbows of foreign competition were felt in the world and domestic markets and reflected in the loss of export markets and rising import penetration; Figure 2.3 tells the story of the UK motor vehicle market'. Thus the profit squeeze for British capital came from competition on the one hand and the power of labour to resist productivity increases on the other. The result was a decline in the profit rate. Capital responded by going overseas or into more profitable ventures such as office development and property speculation. The result was low levels of investment which made much of British industry even more uncompetitive.

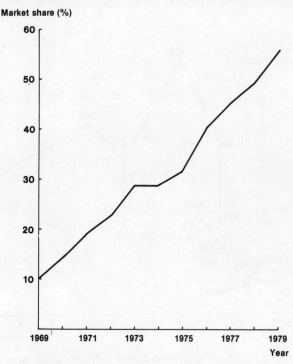

FIGURE 2.3 *Growing import penetration – share of UK motor vehicle market held by imports* SOURCE: UK Motor Manufacturers.

In the early 1970s the British economy was also subject to the shock of high prices of raw material imports. The OPEC decisions to increase the price of oil four-fold marked a fundamental change in the world order. In Britain, and to a varying extent in other countries, organised labour responded to the resultant price increases by asking for wage increases. In this way firms had their costs pushed up by the increased price of imports and by domestic wage inflation. With large price increases, static demand and a growing money supply the result was rapid inflation in the mid 1970s.

If inflation was the curse of the mid 1970s, then unemployment was the plague of the early 1980s. As the world economic system moved into recession, causing a spiral of declining demand, lay-offs and an overall decrease in aggregate demand, the position in Britain was particularly acute because of the lack of competitiveness of domestic companies. Figure 2.4

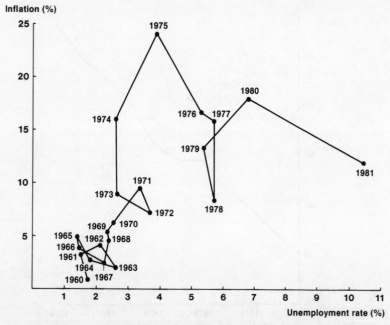

FIGURE 2.4   *UK unemployment against inflation (annual averages)*
SOURCE: *The Economist.*

shows how both inflation and unemployment increased throughout the 1970s. As competition became more intense throughout the 1970s different firms closed, went bankrupt, stopped recruiting and shed labour. The position was made more acute by the high interest rates and a strong pound, a product of the monetarist policies pursued by the Conservative government, all of which made British firms still less competitive on overseas markets. The result was spiralling unemployment (see Figure 2.4) and by late 1982 more than three and a half million people were officially out of work. Much of the increase in unemployment was a direct result of the abrupt decline in manufacturing employment. Between June 1979 and January 1982 approximately 1,300,000 jobs in manufacturing were lost. In that period alone almost one-third of all workers in metal manufacture and a quarter of Britain's textile workers lost their jobs. In the mechanical engineering sector one worker in five was thrown into the dole queue. It is in this context that the controversial term 'de-industrialisation' has come to be used. Blackaby uses the term to refer to a 'progressive failure to achieve a sufficient surplus of exports over imports of manufacturers to keep the economy in external balance at full employment' (Blackaby, 1979, p. 263). Many serious economic forecasters now see a worsening position. Wynne Godley and his associates at the University of Cambridge now talk of three of four million unemployed throughout most of the 1980s, with very little prospect of amelioration, of a countryside scarred with industrial dereliction, of low and deteriorating public services and of a heightening of social and political tension. Although individual forecasts differ in detail, virtually all of them agree that the picture looks bleak.

Political responses

The state assumed a particularly important role in post-war Britain. Government actions became both cause and effect of decisions made in the market-place. Government policy (or non-policy) became the terms of reference of most economic decisions. In this section I will only outline the broad framework of the government's response, and subsequent chapters will flesh out the details where appropriate.

During the boom years of the 1950s and early 1960s economic policy consisted of a fine-tuning of the economy. When unemployment rose 'dangerously' close to 500,000, the Treasury eased credit restrictions, reduced taxes and interest rates – all in order to stimulate the economy. The result was a consumer-led boom. If the rate of inflation was too high or a balance-of-payments deficit appeared once the boom sucked in imports from abroad while export performance was static, taxes and interest rates were increased and hire purchase agreements were made more restrictive. This so-called 'stop–go' policy proved highly detrimental. It only affected aggregate demand and did nothing about supply and the whole system of production. The policy failed to tackle problems of lack of investment and low productivity. Firms would not invest because they thought that the government would not or could not maintain growth. With low expectations and high uncertainty over further demand and hence profitability, capital did not invest to a sufficient extent. In short, the 'stop–go' policy of demand management exacerbated the inherent structural problems of the British economy.

With the ending of the boom and the worsening of the economy came the first attempts to change the prevailing policy orthodoxy. The 1964 Labour government sought to transform the economy in a blaze of technological innovation within a centralised planning framework. A new Department of Economic Affairs was established and the construction of a National Plan was set in motion. The reality, however, was more prosaic. The balance of payments continued to worsen as imports exceeded exports, and in order to close the deficit in 1968 Roy Jenkins, then Chancellor of the Exchequer, devalued the pound (making exports cheaper and imports dearer) and introduced a deflationary budget. The deficit was closed but at the cost of both rising unemployment and inflationary pressure, as workers sought to pay for the most expensive imported goods through higher wage claims.

Throughout the 1970s Britain's economic position worsened. Profits declined, investment was low and unemployment was rising. However, the position of those in work was relatively good. Living standards continued to rise and attempts at controlling prices through restrictions on wages failed as the strength of organised labour brought down both the Conservative government in 1974 and the Labour government of 1979. But the union movement was much less successful in defending the social wage. Cuts in public expenditure have come to be seen by centre and centre-Right parties as important ways out of economic crisis. It was argued that a reduction in the public sector borrowing requirement would reduce the rate of inflation while easing the tax burden on individuals and companies. By freeing resources and allowing incentives, so it is claimed, the pace of economic growth ought to quicken and export performance to improve. Thus throughout the 1960s and 1970s public policy measures were fashioned largely in response to demands for public expenditure cuts. Sometimes the policy was simply one of continuing more or less as before but reducing levels of expenditure. At other times it involved a wholesale reorientation of policy as, for example, the shift in housing policy from comprehensive redevelopment to much cheaper improvement programmes or the change in the inner city programme from an emphasis on welfare to a commitment to stimulating economic growth.

As the 1970s turned into the 1980s and unemployment continued to rise economic matters loomed even larger on the political agenda. It is sometimes difficult to believe that the Conservative party fought the 1979 election on the failure of the Labour government to shorten the dole queues. But the basic issues are clear enough. In social democracies unemployment involves a loss of perceived rights. The post-war consensus had been based on full employment, and jobs were part of the bundle of goods and services obtained in the post-war social contract. Not to have a job was thus to be deprived of an essential right. The onset of mass employment and the continuing failure of the old policies and parties to do anything about reversing economic decline led to a political polarisation within the major parties.

On the Right, there was the rise of Thatcherism. Throughout the 1970s Right-wing thinking was resuscitated and the defeat of Edward Heath's government and the continuing decline in Britain's economic fortunes gave added impetus to the sort of Right-wing strategies given intellectual credibility by commentators like Friedman (1977) and Hayek (1982). The victory of Margaret Thatcher in the Conservative party leadership race in 1975 was both an indication of the changing balance of power within the Conservative party and a further tipping of the scales to the Right. Thatcherism has three main elements:

(1) *A belief in market forces.* The aim of the Conservative government which came to power in 1979 was to reinstatè the workings of the free market in order to ensure economic vitality. Creeping state invervention ('statism') was to be halted and this was to involve both privatisation and the more general rolling-back of the frontiers of state involvement in economy and society.

(2) *A belief in 'sound money'.* The Conservative government's strategy depended on the monetarist thesis that controlling the money supply would squeeze out inflation; the main method was to be an increase in interst rates. Both (1) and (2) could be combined in a concentrated attempt to reduce public expenditure.

(3) *Cutting down the power of the trade unions.* The Conservative government believed that the ability of the unions to maintain high wages in the face of falling productivity was a major reason for Britain's economic decline. The solution was to reduce union power through legislation.

In practice the first Thatcher government increased interest rates and pursued a deflationary policy. Firms were squeezed between falling demand, high interest rates and a high exchange rate. Policy was deliberately aimed at making industry more prcductive through competition forcing weaker firms to the wall and thus disciplining the workforce through high unemployment. The effect on industrial output and unemployment was marked. The increase in unemployment was greater in Britain than in most advanced capitalist countries. In December 1982 unemployment rates were as follows – Britain 13 per cent, United States 10 per cent, France 8 per cent, the Federal Republic of Germany 7 per cent. The Thatcher experiment was probably responsible for about half that level, the rest being caused by the world depression and technological redundancies.

Thatcherism had captured much of the traditional Conservative rhetoric and focused it on some of the more dismal aspects of the experience of contemporary social democracy – the bureaucratisation of the welfare state, the unsavoury aspects of union power and high taxation. Thatcherism did not go completely unchallenged in the Tory party. Those left in the middle by the 'great moving Right show' (Hall, 1979) voiced their disapproval. But quietly. The fear of the Left and increasingly the Social Democratic Party (SDP)/Liberal Alliance made Conservative critics raise their disapproval in muted tones.

The immediate response by the Left was a bout of breast-beating over its past performance. If the Conservatives were ashamed of their part in the growing statism of British society, then some in the Labour party were embarrassed by its continuing commitment to capitalism. Successive post-war Labour governments have done little to change the basic structure of inequality, restricted opportunities or the power of capital. Advances have been made, of course, but for the most part they have been small-scale and limited. More important in the long term, however, was that Thatcherism had questioned the post-war consensus about the nature of the welfare state. The deeper response of Labour Party activists was a Leftward shift in attitudes to the mixed economy. The *Alternative Economic Strategy* emerged from this course (Labour Party, 1981). It suggested that a future Labour government should impose import controls, reduce exchange rates, borrow greater amounts to finance a whole series of public expenditure programmes for creating jobs and building houses, factories and roads. Planning agreements would be signed with major companies and the central–local state relation would be put on a less permissive basis, allowing radical local authorities greater leeway. A significant new feature was the attempt to extend democracy both at the workplace and in the community through workers' councils and tenants' associations, in order to change a top-down society to a bottom-up one. Within the party itself the response of the rank and file was to secure greater power. There was a nagging suspicion held by many of its activists that successive Labour governments had 'sold their socialist birthright' for City respectability and Treasury ortho-doxy. To gain greater control over parliamentary represen-tation, therefore, the activists sought to introduce mandatory reselection of MPs. By this method they hoped to ensure that full-blooded socialist policies would be implemented.

It is a peculiar British irony that as unemployment rose and the fear of social unrest grew the biggest new party to be created since 1945 should be not one of the extreme Right or extreme Left but an avowedly centrist one. It used to be a fundamental tenet of political science and political history that rising unemployment would lead to extremist groups gaining popular credibility. Yet the relationship in Britain of the late 1970s and early 1980s was much more subtle. At the mass level unemployment was leading to political apathy not political activism. The signs of unrest were not in the form of extreme parties but in 'violent, random, delinquent protest, a *Clockwork Orange* world rather than one of political stirrings' (Crick, 1981, p. 2). Radicalisation was occurring within the existing parties as the Left and Right wings of the Labour and Conservative parties respectively gained ascendancy. In one sense the birth of the SDP and the growth of the SDP/Liberal Alliance was a continuation of the centrist strand in British politics nurtured in the 1950s and 1960s by a growing economy which seemed to allow rising expectations without generating conflict. As economic growth faltered and the two major parties shunted to the Left and Right the SDP and the SDP/Liberal Alliance represented the band of politicians stranded in the middle. Support for the Alliance was over-whelmingly from the middle-income groups. Most of its supporters had little previous experience of political activism and their past allegiances were to the seemingly conflict-free 'good times' generated by the post-war economic expansion. The newest party represented a continuation of past trends in a world and national economy which were radically altered. In short, it was a party of capitalism, peopled by social democrats, supported by the middle class but with a mildly socialist rhetoric. It was an attempt to measure up to contemporary issues without the burden or the commitment of past ideo-logies. It was an issue-related, conflict-avoidance method of coping with the British economic crisis.

Emerging tensions

The political responses were only one manifestation of the ending of the post-war boom and the consequent fission in the social democratic compromise. Tensions arose elsewhere. These have been crudely characterised in Figure 2.5, based on the work of Habermas (1976) and O'Connor (1973), as a series of crises. The *economic crisis* has been one of declining profits for capital and rising unemployment for labour. The crisis has been articulated inside the factory between management, seeking to improve productivity by shedding labour and introducing new work practices, and the trade union movement attempting to protect members' interests. The hand of capital has been strengthened by the recession with its lengthening dole queues. Management calls for 'responsibility' in wage bargaining and work practice agreements take on great potency when there are over three million unemployed. However, it is not simply the absolute level of unemployment that is an important consideration, but its rate of growth. If the unemployment rate steadies, even at a high rate, then those in employment have less to fear about job loss. In early 1983, for example, there was some indication when the rate of unemployment was levelling off that labour, particularly in the car manufacturing industry, was not so compliant as several years previously when the rate of increase in job loss was much higher. It would seem that unemployment as a technique to discipline labour only works when the rate of increase is constant or ever-increasing.

Tension occurs within the political arena of the state. The state becomes the scene of conflict as it is on the one hand the main single agent entrusted with securing conditions for profit

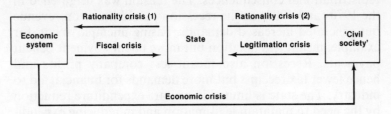

FIGURE 2.5   *Emerging tensions*

maintenance and improvement but on the other it is, in liberal democracies, also charged with maintaining mass support.

Three crises can arise. The growing intervention of the state involves a huge administrative input with consequent potential for a *rationality crisis*, i.e. a failure to produce the correct decisions given the large number of different signals from competing capitals and sections of labour. The state can and does make mistakes. A rationality crisis type 1 occurs when the state fails to regulate the economy. This has been apparent in failures to stop both inflation and unemployment increasing. Given present knowledge and disposition it seems that to tackle one is to avoid the other. A rationality crisis type 2 occurs in social welfare policies and is apparent for example in the failure of the education system to produce people with enough skills for a shrinking job market. These two types are closely related as economic policies have social welfare implications and welfare policies impinge on economic considerations. When and if the state makes too many mistakes then a rationality crisis may turn into a crisis of legitimation. A *legitimation crisis* can occur when the state cannot maintain a sufficient degree of mass loyalty to secure the orderly reproduction of social and political life. In Britain there is not a widescale legitimation crisis. There has been a steady decline in support for the two main political parties but increasing levels of apathy do not constitute a major constitutional crisis. The crisis is more concentrated in specific sections of the population: the unemployed, the young, the black and all those marginalised in a declining economy. Much of the tension within the state is expressed in terms of taxation and spending. A *fiscal crisis* of the state can occur when expenditure outruns revenue and the gap can only be closed at the expense of major redistributional consequences. The tension was heightened in the 1970s and 1980s as the recession placed limits on revenue but generated increased demands. Rising unemployment, for example, meant less taxation but more unemployment benefit payments. Recession also meant less company profits and hence fewer tax receipts but more demands for financial aid to industry. The state is limited in welfare expenditure reduction by the need to maintain legitimation and in reducing expenditure associated with capital accumulation by the need to secure the position of capital. Cutbacks take the line of least resistance as expenditure reduction is made in so-called 'unproductive' investments and 'wasteful' welfare programmes and in attempts to improve the efficiency of public investments. The mismatch between revenue and expenditure is often expressed differently at different levels of government. In both North America and Britain the gap is greatest at the urban level. The fiscal crisis of the city is the spatial manifestation of the fiscal crisis of the state.

The dilemma of limited financial resources and growing demands is faced by all countries. Each society has its particular fiscal crisis. Lester Thurow's (1981) specific description of the United States as a zero-sum society in which no group can gain except at the expense of others is a good general description of all advanced capitalist countries. In Britain, however, the tensions are particularly acute because of the scale and pace of economic decline and the relative strength of organised labour and community groups. As Austin Mitchell notes:

> Britain is steadily becoming Europe's scrounger, a mean, divided, creaking society in which blame is the general chorus and the political struggle is worse than the zero-sum which dominates the politics of nil growth. With actual decline the struggle becomes sub-zero, sub-sum, super-nasty. (Crick, 1981, p. 50)

The tensions are greatest in the inner city locations of our major conurbations. Here the failure of the market to provide jobs and the failure of the state to provide enough 'welfare' combine with an alienated population to produce the explosive mixture of social unrest and rioting. The urban discontent of the long summer of 1981 was the embodiment of the most extreme trends in contemporary British society.

In the following chapters I will seek to show the specific nature of the emerging tensions, the response of the main actors and the unfolding consequences of their actions. I will consider the response of capital, the concern of communities and the nature of the state's counter to dwindling resources and high demands.

3
The Response of Capital

In late capitalist societies, goods are produced by firms to be sold at a profit, and financial institutions lend money and invest in order to secure high and safe returns. A useful distinction can be drawn for present purposes between an *industrial capital* which is concerned with the production of commodities and *finance capital* which is concerned with the lending of money and investment. The two are obviously interlinked. Industrialists often seek funds to build a new factory, pay off debts and buy raw materials before the cycle of production is completed, so that for industrial capital credit from the finance institutions bridges the gap between the production and realisation of commodities. The two forms of capital are represented by different institutional forms: industrial capital is represented by (in particular) the Confederation of British Industry (CBI) while finance capital has a less direct but nonetheless real representation in the power of the City, the Bank of England and the Treasury. Their twin interests do not always coincide of course; thus the CBI wants a cheap pound in order to make exports more competitive and access to easy credit in order to restructure the labour process, while sections of finance capital concerned with attracting overseas money may want high interest rates and a strong pound. It has been a consistent finding of successive studies of the post-war British economy that the interests of industrial capital have generally been sacrificed to those of finance capital.

But it is important not to draw too sharp a distinction. Both are concerned with increasing profits and their operations often overlap. Banks and pension funds have interests in British industry and the financial sector helps channel industrial firms' funds into sectors yielding high rates of return. In the context of a well-organised working class, it is the similarities of interest between industrial and finance capital that are important. Both fear a strong interventionist state in

28

the hands of a militant Labour party and backed by the big trade unions. The terms 'industrial capital' and 'finance capital' thus need to be used with care, and they are meant to represent different but related facets of capital.

Industrial capital

The decision-making context for industrial capital has been the decline in the profitability of traditional domestic industrial production. The response has been to restructure and invest in more profitable sectors. As in other countries the restructuring, often aided by the government, has had to fight against union resistance, but in Britain the battle has been particularly acute because of the interrelated features of high labour militancy and a slow-growth economy. To some extent, there has been less willingness to take up the fight because of the ease with which funds can be moved elsewhere. The relatively efficient financial sector and the lack of effective restrictions on investment flows have widened the choices open to industrial capital. But this flexibility is also a function of the characteristics of industrial capital itself.

Characteristics

The most important characteristics of industrial capital in Britain are its size, level of diversification and international dimension. Let us consider each in turn

Size and concentration. One of the most important features has been the growing concentration of industrial production: five firms or fewer control 91 per cent of the market in motor vehicles, 77 per cent in electrical engineering and 92 per cent in chemicals. Business in contemporary Britain is truly big business, and is dominated by the giant corporations. This growing concentration – which can be defined as 'the increase in the collective dominance of a relatively small group of giant firms at the level of the economy and of specific sectors'

(Aaronovitch *et al.*, 1981, p. 264) – is common in most advanced capitalist countries, but the decline of the small firms is more marked in the United Kingdom. The concentration of industrial capital has been advancing throughout most of this century, but it has become more marked as a consequence of the merger movements since the mid 1950s, the preference of the financial institutions to lend to the large (= less risky) firms and the modernisation strategies of the state.

The fact that certain sectors of the British economy are dominated by a small number of large firms has a number of important consequences. First, it limits the operation of market competition. When a few large firms dominate the market then competition can very quickly turn into implicit collusion, because all firms are quick to pass on cost increases to the consumer but fail to pass on price reductions caused by improvements in production or falls in material costs. The rise of oligopolies signals the decline in the operation of the competitive market. Things will of course vary from sector to sector. Where entry costs are large and the sector is shielded from foreign incursions then internal competition will be minimal. But where entry costs are low and foreign firms are more in evidence then competition may be more apparent. Second, the firms themselves become important figures in the public policy landscape. They wield considerable economic weight and any government must consider them in formulating and implementing public policies. Stuart Holland has coined the term 'meso-economic power' to refer to the rise of these big corporations. The interests of capital have always been represented in British governments, of course, but now the power of specific organisations and the effects of their investment, purchasing and management decisions ensures specific firms a central place in government decision-making. It is not only that governments have to listen, they may also have to act. Upper Clyde Shipbuilders, Rolls-Royce, Chrysler and British Leyland were some of the biggest casualties in Britain's post-war economic decline, but the government of the day bailed them out not so much because they were lame ducks but rather because they were big lame ducks who squawked. Their demise would have affected a large number of suppliers, creditors and workers.

Diversification. The modern corporation is not only big it is a multi-product enterprise. Large companies have diversified their operations. The merger movement since the mid 1950s has partly been an attempt by successful companies to buy into other sectors. It was more feasible for firms with cash to buy existing companies with existing lines of business than to start afresh. It also made good fiscal sense. In the British tax system the costs and losses of acquirement can be offset against the acquiring companies' profits. The general trend has thus been for the larger companies to swallow up the smaller ones. The net result has been to increase the level of concentration. Most major corporations now have a number of interests in different sectors of the economy. Risk is spread wider while the multiplicity of holdings allows the company to respond rapidly to variations in profitability. Capital can be withdrawn from unprofitable sectors and quickly switched to more profitable ones, all under the same corporate umbrella.

The international dimension. The major British companies are multinational. Just over 20 per cent of the largest multi-nationals are British. The relative position of overseas production in the British economy is highlighted in Figure 3.1. The international dimension is an important characteristic of British corporations. (Buckley and Pearce, 1977). In the nineteenth century the British economy was the most powerful and competitive in the world. British companies sought to set up branch plants overseas while British capital was used to finance the industrial revolution in many countries. The result was a large world-wide web of interests emanating from Britain. This interest has persisted and, as we shall see, increased.

The response

The end of the post-war economic boom marked a sharp decline in the fortunes of many British firms. Undercut by foreign competition in the home market and unable to increase orders abroad they face major problems. The response of capital has been four-fold.

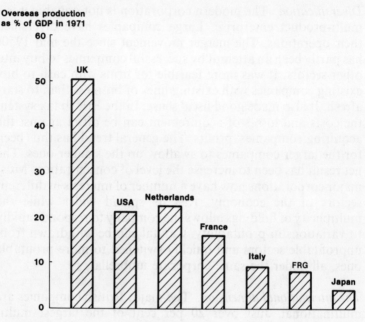

FIGURE 3.1   *Overseas production of major capitalist countries*

SOURCE: Buckley and Pearce (1977).

(1) *Not investing.* Since profit levels have fallen one response of capital has been not to invest in manufacturing. This has not occurred to the same extent with Britain's more successful economic competitors. By 1975 gross fixed capital formation as per cent of GDP was 17.8 in the United Kingdom compared to 23.0 in the Federal Republic of Germany and 32.1 in Japan. One result of this poor investment record has been the decline in British productivity. As foreign firms have invested in more efficient factories and more modern equipment, so goods produced in the less efficient British factories using out-of-date plant have become more expensive and hence less competitive in the world market. The lack of investment is one of many causes behind the severity of the current recession in Britain. Industrial capital has been able to avoid investing in relatively unprofitable enterprises because firms are large, diversified and internationalised so that they can move funds quickly and easily to more profitable alternatives.

(2) *Investing abroad*. One response of British firms to low profits at home has been to invest abroad. Direct investment abroad involves investment by UK companies in the operation of their overseas branches, subsidiaries and associates. As Figure 3.2 demonstrates, there has been a dramatic rise in direct investment overseas. As profits and capital investment in the United Kingdom have declined so overseas investment by UK firms has increased. There are many reasons for this outward drift in investment. Firms set up factories and offices

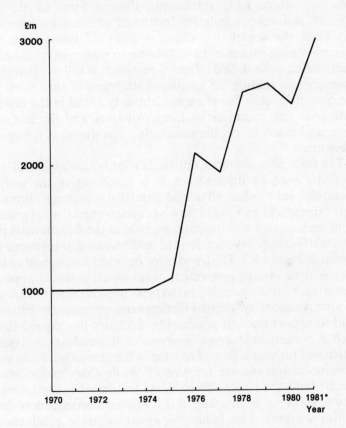

FIGURE 3.2   *UK private direct investment overseas*

* Three quarters only.

SOURCE: Treasury.

overseas in order to jump tarrif barriers, to comply with regulative legislation affecting foreign enterprises, to break into overseas markets directly and to compete more favourably with overseas competitors. However, the argument that there is a necessity to invest in this way is partly undermined by the changing distribution of overseas investment. While in 1962 only 13.4 per cent of total outward investment went to Western Europe, by 1976 this figure had increased to 27.5 per cent. Thus a significant proportion of overseas investment was going to countries where EEC agreements allowed firms to export directly. A further significant feature of overseas investment has been the search for cheap sources of labour. Many manufacturing processes have become so routinised that only semi-skilled or unskilled labour is required. It follows that the main criteria guiding the locational strategies of such firms is the cost of labour. The cheapest labour is found in the newly industrialising countries in Latin America and South-East Asia, and much recent manufacturing investment is going to these areas.

The flow of investment outwards is only one aspect of an economy such as Britain's which is firmly set in the world economy. Like other advanced capitalist countries, Britain also experiences an inward flow of foreign capital as overseas firms seek to gain a corresponding hold in the British market. The relationship between inward and outward investment is shown in Figure 3.3. The trend is for outward investment to be greater than inward investment, from which it would appear that British firms operating in overseas markets tend to export productive capacity whereas foreign firms operating in Britain tend to export finished goods. The Treasury has argued that such a pattern of overseas investment is building up assets which will provide a flow of income in the years ahead, but the question arises: income for whom? While shareholders may benefit (and the larger shareholders will benefit most), there would seem to be marked distributional consequences for British workers. The failure to invest in home production makes British-based manufacturing units less productive. The ageing stock in major companies will be concentrated in Britain while the more modern, more efficient plants will be overseas. When competition increases and the recession causes

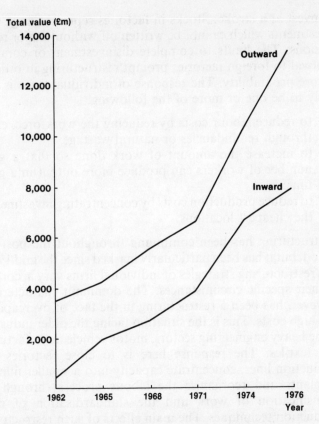

FIGURE 3.3 *Outward and inward direct capital stake**

* (Book value of fixed assets + current assets) − (current liabilities + long-term liabilities of overseas subsidiaries and branches).

SOURCE: Derived from data in Dunning, J. (1979) 'The UK's International Investment Position in the Mid-1970s', *Lloyds Bank Review*, April.

restructuring it is British workers who will lose their jobs. The net effect will be to disinvest capital from Britain, lessen the demand for labour in Britain and hence increase unemployment.

(3) *Restructuring.* There are limits to the process of disinvestment and overseas investment. Industrial capital cannot

disinvest at a stroke. Stocks in factories represent huge fixed investments which cannot be written off without major repercussions. The limits to complete disinvestment or complete removal to foreign factories prompt restructuring in order to restore profitability. The response of individual firms is then likely to be one or more of the following:

(i) to reduce labour costs by reducing the workforce, either through redundancies or natural wastage;
(ii) to increase the amount of work done so that a given number of workers can produce more output in a given time;
(iii) to reduce production costs by concentrating investment in the cheapest locations.

Restructuring has been continuing throughout the post-war period, but it has been particularly marked since the mid 1960s. The restructuring strategies of individual firms vary according to their specific circumstances. The dominant characteristic, however, has been a restructuring in the face of overcapacity and high costs. This is the situation facing the older industries in the heavy engineering sectors, motor vehicle manufacturing and textiles. The response here is to close factories and production lines, concentrate capacity into a smaller number of plants and reorganise the labour process through the intensification of work and the standardisation of mass production techniques. The main effects of such restructuring are closures and job losses. Manufacturing employment in Britain has decreased from 7.9 million in 1971 to 5.9 million in 1981.

By its very nature restructuring implies a change in the relationship between capital and labour. At the level of individual plants, restructuring in most cases involves job losses. In the case of the twelve largest plants in Merseyside for example, which together employ 50 per cent of manufacturing workers in the region, between 1966 and 1975 the demand for labour declined from 35,600 to 25,500. The shedding of labour has not involved factory closures, but it has involved increased workloads: less people were doing the same amount of work.

Throughout the 1960s union response to job losses was

limited by the existence of full exployment and rising real wages. Whereas losses may have led to problems in particular localities, the national picture was masked by the creation of jobs in the service sector, and particularly the public service sector, while increased workloads were tied into productivity agreements and higher wages. The early and mid 1970s marked a subsequent change. Full employment was becoming a thing of the past and in a declining economy job losses in particular firms meant a net job loss. On the one hand union resistance was stiffened by the lack of employment alternatives, but on the other hand increasing unemployment also tempered union resistance. It is difficult to be militant when the dole queues are long and growing. Moreover, the hyper-mobility of capital weakened labour, which has been better organised and more responsive at the local rather than the national level.

But it has not been a story of total acquiescence on the part of organised labour. The response has been two-fold. First, there has been an increase in sit-ins and occupations of factories and plants scheduled for closure. The biggest and perhaps the most successful was the shipyard workers' response on Clydeside. In 1972 the Upper Clyde Shibuilders (UCS) decided to close down four yards. The shop stewards staged a sit-in and what later turned into a work-in. Eventually the government was called in and they arranged for an American company to take over the yards, albeit at reduced manning levels. The UCS became a symbol and model for worker resistance and it was copied with varying success throughout the country. If the sit-ins are the set pieces, the second response has been the less dramatic 'guerilla warfare' of bargaining at plant level to limit workloads and management control. Although some union successes have been recorded, the overwhelming picture in the current recession is the strengthening of the hand of capital. Just as organised labour gained during the years of full employment so it has lost in the present era of high unemployment.

The consequences of restructuring in the low-growth economy during the recession are many. But perhaps the main one, as I have indicated, is increasing unemployment (see Figure 3.4). Firms are reducing their labour force by sacking workers or not replacing those made redundant, retiring or

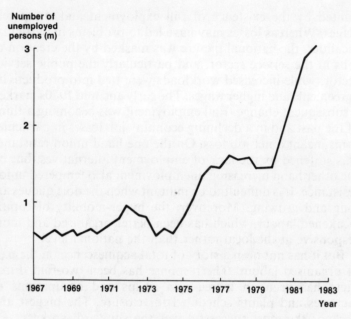

FIGURE 3.4   *Registered unemployed in the United Kingdom*

SOURCE: Department of Employment.

leaving for other employment. Firms retain their skilled
workers for as long as is possible but refuse to recruit once they
leave. The effect is to limit the job opportunities of young
people coming onto the job market. In the current recession,
therefore, it is scarcely surprising that youth unemployment
should be such a significant feature. In 1982 almost 1.25 million
of the officially declared unemployed were aged under 25 and
this figure did not include the 280,000 people on youth
opportunity programmes. The position of school-leavers is
particularly actute and by 1983 only one in three school-leavers
was likely to find a job. The unskilled and semi-skilled are
particularly badly hit by the introduction of labour-saving
machines, but so too are the skilled workers in the declining
manufacturing sectors. The age of the microchip is the age of
technological redundancy. There is of course no inevitable

connection between technological developments and unemployment: everything depends on the way technology is used. In a perfect world the introduction of new machines would release people for other jobs and more meaningful leisure. But we live in a world where machines are used to increase profits rather than to realise the fullness of human potential.

Unemployment has varied throughout the country. On the regional scale there is a division between the tepid 'sunbelt' stretching from East Anglia through the South-East to the South-West, where unemployment rates are between 10 and 30 per cent below the national average, and the rest of the country where unemployment rates are between 4 and 55 per cent above the national average (see Figure 3.5). Even so, all regions have seen an increase in unemployment, although there have been some changes in their relative positions. The selected regions shown in Table 3.1 allow us to identify the three main trends. First, the South-East has maintained the relatively good employment position which it has enjoyed since the war. Unemployment has increased, to be sure, but not so much as in the rest of the country. Second, there has been some convergence in unemployment rates, as shown in figures for Scotland and the North. This is not an improvement on their part, however, as absolute levels of unemployment are growing, but merely an indication of the more widespread nature of unemployment. Third, some formerly prosperous areas of the country have experienced both an absolute and a relative deterioration in their levels of employment. The case of the West Midlands is particularly marked. Here the boom region of the 1960s has become the problem region of the 1980s as the manufacturing base has been destroyed by a mixture of foreign competition and lack of effective demand. The increasing unemployment is one consequence of the growing important penetration in the motor vehicle sector. The metal economies of the Midlands have been severely damaged in the present recession. With a high proportion of young people, a product of the immigration of young families in the 1960s, and a heavy reliance on manufacturing, the West Midlands are facing particular problems of higher unemployment in general and youth unemployment in particular. One of Coventry's leading pop groups, The Specials, reached number 1 in the charts in

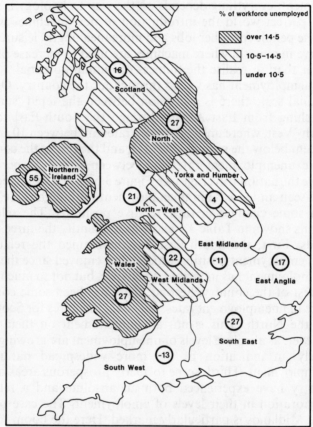

FIGURE 3.5   *Unemployment by region**

* Circled figures indicate unemployment rates relative to UK average (% above or below) in January 1982.

Britain in July 1981 with their single, *Ghost Town*. The lyrics were redolent with images of youth unemployment:

> This town is coming like a ghost town
> Why must the youth fight against themselves
> Government leaving youth on the shelf
> This town is coming like a ghost town

TABLE 3.1 *Unemployment by selected regions*

Region	Unemployment rate as % of UK average		
	1965	1975	1982
South-East	63	69	67
Scotland	215	127	116
North	185	146	127
West Midlands	68	99	122
UK average unemployment rate (%)	1.5	5.3	11.7

SOURCE: Department of Employment.

> No job to be found in this country
> Can't go on no more, people getting angry
> This town is coming like a ghost town.

But these regional figures mask considerable intraregional variations. The figures for the South-East, for example, mask the high unemployment rates in inner London where each borough has unemployment rates higher than the national average. Similarly, the high unemployment figures for the West Midlands reflect the bleak position of Coventry rather than the affluent suburbs of Solihull. In general, unemployment is greatest in the inner city areas and the larger conurbations where there are pools of unskilled labour and the impact of restructuring has been in the form of closed factories and reduced labour forces. The net growth that has occurred in the more favoured regions has been in the freestanding cities, small towns and rural areas.

In contemporary Britain, then, the dominant economic story has been one of deindustrialisation as manufacturing jobs have been lost. In the favoured towns and cities of Britain's 'sunbelt' the loss of old manufacturing jobs has been partly offset by jobs in the new 'sunrise' industries and by continuing service employment. Elsewhere few new jobs have been created. Throughout the 1960s and 1970s service-based employment took up some of the slack especially in the public sector. But as the recession has increased and government has reduced public spending, so unemployment has grown and the collapse of the manufacturing base has not been matched by the service sector soaking up the unemployed. De-industrialisation has meant growing unemployment. The aim of most local authorities has been to create more employment, but in the worst-affected areas local authority action is severely constrained by the level of job loss in the private sector. As a report in the *Guardian* noted:

> Liverpool has an unemployment rate of 18.6% . . . . The city council's response has been to promise a new sports centre, costing £2m, and more local work training schemes. 'The city has created about 4,500 jobs in less than 2½ years,' said Sir Trevor. 'But when you loose them at a rate of 10,000 a year then the council's action is merely a drop in the bucket.' (*Guardian,* 3 March 1982).

(4) *Redirecting the state.* The fourth major response of indus-trial capital has been the attempt to (re)direct government policies. This has taken the form of three main prompts:

  (i) directing government taxation and expenditure;
 (ii) providing the 'right' climate for industrial relations;
(iii) creating more business for private industry.

The prompting has come from key decision-makers whose interests span directorships and political positions and from the representative organisations of industrial capital in Britain. There is nothing new in the lobbying of government by capital. What is different is the balance of power and the precise nature of the demands: with three and a half million unemployed organised labour is weakened and capital is strengthened, and the demands of industry have been articulated through the supply-side economics which have gained currency with the ending of the long post-war boom.

  (i) *Paying less and getting more.* Companies in Britain have been successful in minimising the amount of corporate tax-ation. The real level of company taxation in Britain has consistently fallen since 1950 (see King, 1975). Between 1955 and 1965 the proportion of taxation raised from companies fell from 21 to 11 per cent. This trend has continued. There are two consequences. First, it has offset the fall in profits. The crisis of profitability has been minimised by a continual decline in the level of company taxation. Second, with the rise in public expenditure the burden of taxation has fallen on wage-earners rather than companies, on income rather than capital. The power of the wealthy, the owners and controllers of companies has been translated into a regressive tax system. One study of taxation in Britain came to the conclusion:

> . . . the increased demands for public revenue have lead to a massive increase in the level of direct taxation since the war. The burden of this increased taxation has not been spread equally between different social groups, but has been concentrated on the recipients of earned income – ordinary wage earners and salary earners. Amongst those dependent on earned income, we have also seen that the top income groups have enjoyed a reduction in their tax contributions at the expense of those at the lower end. Finally, amongst the mass of ordinary wage earners who have borne the brunt of the increased taxation, the low paid and those with families have been called upon to contribute a disproportionate share. (Field *et al.*, 1977, p. 29)

The poor economic performance of the British economy has produced a climate favourable to theories which stress the need to help industry. High inflation and spiralling unemployment dented the Keynesian orthodoxy. New and refurbished alternatives then appeared, in which public taxation and expenditure played on important role. In supply-side economies, increases in taxation and high taxation are considered damaging to entrepreneurship. The model used is one which connects tax reductions to economic resuscitation. This theory provides an elegant excuse for greed; it gives a theoretical justification for giving more to the rich. In the monetarist variant, public expenditure was seen as an underlying cause of economic problems. In order to spend, so the monetarists argued, government either borrowed (which raised interest rates and crowded out investment in the private market) or printed money (and hence caused inflation). The prevailing economic ideology in contemporary Britain has begun to see public expenditure as something to be cut. This has been true of both Labour and Conservative governments. In his 'letter of intent' to the International Monetary Fund in 1976 Denis Healey agreed to reduce such expenditure, and in the Conservative government's White Paper of 1979 it was plainly stated: 'higher public expenditure cannot any longer be allowed to precede, and thus prevent growth in the private sector' (Treasury, 1979, p. 2). Reductions in public expenditure were not canvassed across the board. The greatest savings were to be made in the welfare state expenditures, while aid to the private sector was to be left largely untouched. The fiscal crisis of the state thus led to demands for restructuring public expenditure but the constellation of powerful interests dictated the direction of the restructuring. A lighter taxation load was to be used to stimulate and aid the private sector.

It can be seen then, that economic theories which hold sway in contemporary Britain now match business interests, in that the need to cut company taxation and aid private industry is taken as symptomatic of good government practice. A mixture of business lobbying and economic recession has made a neat dovetailing between the interests of industrial capital and the state in the realm of public expenditure.

(ii) *Providing the 'right' climate.* In order to restructure effectively, companies need a high degree of control over labour. In order to keep costs down and profits up they want wage claims and price increases to be kept low. In Britain, however, industrial capital has not sought to maintain its power over the workforce through incomes policies or through direct control of legal sanctions. Incomes policies can easily become part of a wider strategy of controlling profits, prices and investment strategies, and companies do not want to be in the front line of taking their own workforce to court: so firms have sought to shift the onus of legal action onto the state. This has been attempted through a series of legislative measures designed to regulate industrial relations, from Labour's *In Place of Strife* to the Conservative's Employment Acts of 1980 and 1982 all of which had to reckon with the power of the trade unions. Union activity in Britain brought down Heath's Conservative government in 1974 and was instrumental in Callaghan's Labour government losing the 1979 election. But recent years have seen a marked change in the balance of power. Under the social contract between the unions and the Labour government of 1974–9, for example, the labour movement gained a lot. Taken together, the Trade Unions and Labour Relations Act of 1974 and the Employment Protection Act of 1976 gave:

● protection against dismissal
● increased redundancy payments
● paid maternity leave
● union immunity from common law action
● improved arbitration through the Advisory, Conciliation and Arbitration Service (ACAS).

By the end of the 1970s, however, the balance of power was shifting. The external economy was strengthening the hand of capital as the high levels of unemployment had begun to mediate wage claims. The fear of unemployment shifted the capital–labour balance. The political climate was moving in the same direction. With the return of the Conservatives in 1979 came a government explicitly committed to reducing the power of the unions; their 1980 and 1982 Employment Acts:

● reduced union picketing powers
● made unions liable for damages in the event of support for secondary actions
● ensured periodic reballoting of the closed shop.

(iii) *Creating more space for the private sector.* As companies have struggled to maintain and find business in a shrinking market, many of them have cast their eyes rather enviously on the privileged position of state-run enterprises. As the recession has deepened and widened, private companies have sought to move into sectors previously secured by the state. The methods used to open up the public sector have varied from demands for the public issue of shares, the sale of physical assets of state-run enterprises and the contracting out of public services by central government and local authorities. These policies of privatisation have been vigorously lobbied for by industrial capital and given legislative form by the 1979 Conservative government in a series of acts ranging from the Local Government, Planning and Land Act of 1980 which made the local authorities contract out building work, to the Transport Bill which sought to diminish the monopoly power of the National Bus Company.

To see something of the pressures for privatisation, let us take the example of the building industry. Most local authorities have their own building departments called Direct Labour Organisations (DLOs) which are concerned with building but particularly with maintenance work on local authority projects. In the early and mid 1970s the local authorities had to use the DLOs to an increasing extent because the private builders were finding more lucrative business both in the domestic property boom and in the expanding overseas market especially the Middle East. With the fall of the Shah, the drop in the Organisation of Petroleum-Exporting Countries (OPEC) receipts and the contraction of work at home came the pressure on private builders to find more contracts. The builders sought to muscle in on the work of the DLOs and a vigorous anti-DLO campaign was mounted at both national and local levels. Given the close ties between the Conservative party and the building industry it was no surprise that incoming Conservative government of 1979 sought to turn this lobbying into direct action. In a series of circulars, the Department of Environment advised local authorities to put more of their maintenance jobs out to contract and required DLOs to make a 5 per cent return on capital, a return which building firms had not achieved in the past eight years.

This example shows that the demand for privatisation is really a response to both declining profits and shrinking markets. It has taken the form of calls for limiting state involvement, privatising specific services and making the public sector run within stringent guidelines. There has always been pressure for privatisation because small firms in particular have always felt vulnerable against the larger state enterprises with huge financial resources. But the more intense and recent successful campaigning has come from the bigger and more powerful companies as state involvement has grown and the recession has deepened. It was implemented by the Thatcher government which saw it as a way of rewarding their allies, disciplining the workforce and, in the peculiar tenets of Thatcherism, securing greater freedom through private enterprise. The extremes of privatisation expressed by the Conservative government were highlighted in the plans for the National Enterprise Board (NEB) which is a body used by the government to invest in companies. The NEB had to satisfy that private sector finance was not available before it could invest and once it had done so the companies or subsidiaries had to be returned to private ownership once they became viable. The state was not allowed to make a profit or to be effective or efficient.

There is not one set of clear policy guidelines which private industry can set government in a mixed economy where there are powerful unions. Crouch (1979) notes the ambivalant nature of the relationship between private capital and the state:

In general employers want a government which keeps out of industry (but bails out, on industry's terms, firms which get into difficulties); which does not allow the level of unemployment to get too low (but keeps the economy buoyant); which keeps control of unions and income growth (but does not get in employers' way when so doing). (pp. 147–8)

A problem for industrial capital has thus been to present a coherent strategy covering a variety of interests. Different companies may be in competition, while there is a pronounced difference between corporations and the small business sector. The big firms work closely with government and often prefer the closed shop as a device for keeping good labour relations, while for the smaller company the state is generator of timewasting forms, a competitor with huge resources and the closed shop an anathema. The difference between ICI and Grunwick is more than just size, for there is a pronounced difference in attitudes towards the state and unions which effect the running of the firms. It is an interesting paradox that while the economic landscape has become dominated more and more by the giants, so the ideology of the Conservative government which came to power in 1979 came to be based very much on the priorities of the small firms. The growth and renewal of small firms is more than just an economic strategy, however: it is an attempt to recreate the conditions of a flourishing, competitive, 'free market'.

It has often been noted that while the lobbying of the labour movement is more public, more direct and more explicit, industrial capital is rarely seen nudging ministers' elbows. This has become less true as the CBI has taken a less opaque role in presenting its case to the public as well as to the government of the day. Moreover, the observation ignores the power of economic reality and social ideology. In a capitalist society private capital is the main generator of jobs, incomes and economic growth. Its power is given by the nature of the economy and its logic is accepted in the cultural fabric of the society. In other words, industrial capital does not lobby all that much, simply because it does not have to. But direct lobbying does occur. As Walter Goldsmith, Director-General of the Institute of Directors, remarked:

> We, more than any others, were responsible for the Tebbit law on trade unions. We have successfully urged the government not to reflate the economy. The National Insurance Surcharge reduction has been clawed back from nationalised industries because we campaigned for that saving of £300m through the government. And without us tax cutting would be dead. (*The Observer*, 21 March 1982)

Business interests are also articulated at the local level. Through the Chamber of Commerce and the constituency Conservative party the interests of small industrial and commercial firms are strongly represented. As at the national level the lobbying has sought to minimise costs and maximise business advantages, but the precise demands are tailored to the circumstances and powers of local government. A typical manifesto is outlined in the five-point plan proclaimed by the Central Scotland Chamber of Commerce in May 1982, which suggested:

 (i) action to halt spiralling costs of local authority services;
 (ii) endeavours to attract incoming industry;

(iii) control over public utilities costs;
(iv) privatising certain local authority services;
 (v) controlling local authority expenditure.

Local businesses want lower rates, more privatisation and cheaper services. There are clearly limits to this lobbying power. The rating system, for example, can only be changed by central government. But local authorities have a degree of autonomy in the way money should be spent. And where Conservatives and local business interests are most keenly represented there is less expenditure on welfare services, more on aiding industry and more schemes for privatising services such as waste disposal formerly under the control of the local authority. The main problem for local authorities in this case is the resistance of public sector unions whose jobs are directly affected. It is not only Conservatives who want to encourage economic growth in general and small firms in particular, however, for the scale of unemployment has attuned most local authorities to the needs of creating jobs, and no self-respecting authority is now without its industrial development officer charged with attracting firms and helping to start up local ones. During a recession more attention is paid to the needs of capital as the main producer of jobs.

Capital has been relatively successful in directing state action to meet its needs. The recession and political events tilted the capital–labour balance. Although the Thatcher government marked a radical shift to the Right and produced an administration more explicitly pro-capital and anti-labour than anything previously seen in the post-war period it was not a sudden aberration. The previous Labour government had also been committed to restructuring public expenditure in order to aid industry and export performance. But the mixture of Thatcherism and the world recession does not herald a complete victory for capital. Although union powers have been blunted by the fear of the dole queue and the nature of Conservative legislation, organised labour is still a powerful force, a force which can only be disciplined with increasing rates of unemployment. In the system of mutual antagonism found between capital and labour in a liberal–democratic mixed economy there can be no out-and-out victors, but only shifts in the balance of power. Anything else would signify a transformation of society.

Finance capital

In Britain there is a highly developed system of markets concerned with the lending and investment of money. The institutions concerned with the channelling of savings into loans and investments are collectively known as finance capital, the City or just plain financial institutions. As used here the terms are interchangeable. A distinction can be drawn between *deposit-taking* institutions, the banks and building societies, and the *investing* institutions of pension funds and insurance companies. The deposit-taking institutions have to attract investors by their rate of return, and the amount they take in depends upon their rate of return. The investing institutions are charged with handling the funds at their disposal to secure and maintain high and safe returns. The tremendous growth in recent years of these institutions is demonstrated in Figure 3.6 while their present size is shown in Table 3.2. The size of the institutions' assets are such that they are important economic agents in their own right. They figure as important elements in national economic accounting and as important interests to which governments must at least refer if not satisfy.

The financial institutions mediate the flow of savings and investment, loans and mortgages, between the different sectors of the economy. The flow of savings into these institutions takes the form of deposits in banks and building societies, policies in insurance companies and contributions to pension fund schemes. The out-flow of money takes the form of loans and mortgages in the personal sector, loans and equity investments into private companies and loans to and purchase of gilts from the government. The main development in the financial markets has been the increase in personal savings. Savings in the personal sector increased from 3.9 per cent of capital gross domestic product (GDP) in 1959 to 10.8 per cent in 1979. This increase came about because of rising real incomes and the increased savings ratio (personal savings as a percentage of personal disposal income increased from 6.4 per cent in 1958–62

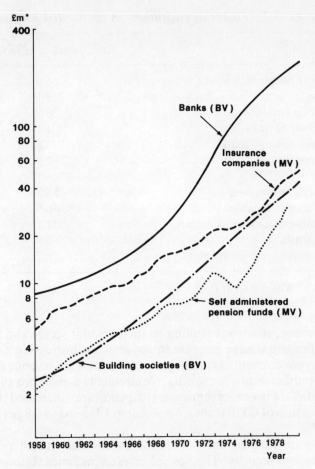

FIGURE 3.6 *Growth of financial institutions*

* End-of-year assets at book value (BV) or market value (MV).

SOURCE: Wilson Report (1980) *Committee to Review the Functioning of Financial Institutions*, Cmnd 7939 (London: HMSO).

to 15 per cent in 1979). The growth of occupational pension schemes and the purchase of insurance policies, all aided by various tax measures, have also produced a huge flow of personal savings into the financial institutions. The other side of the financial equation saw an increase in private company

TABLE 3.2   *Financial institutions in the United Kingdom*

	Total assets in 1978 (£b)
Deposit-taking institutions	266.4
Banks	219.1
Building societies	39.7
National Savings Bank	1.1
Trustee Savings Bank	3.6
Finance houses	2.9
Investing institutions	88.5
Insurance companies	46.8
Self-administered pension funds	31.1
Unit trusts	3.9
Investment trust companies	6.7

SOURCE: Wilson Report (1980).

borrowing, mortgage lending to the personal sector and very significantly a huge increase in government borrowing as the rise in government expenditures went beyond the revenue base. The public sector borrowing requirement, a measure of the shortfall between revenue and expenditure, increased as a proportion of GDP from 2.4 per cent in 1958–62 to 6.8 per cent in 1979.

The institutions are dominated by the calculus of profitability and security. The flow of investment funds follows the rhythm of profitability while loans move to the beat of security. As an example, Figure 3.7 shows the changing proportion of insurance company investment by different sectors. The rise and fall follows the pattern of relative profitability. Given the nature of British society – and we will define the specific aspects where appropriate – the flows of investment and loans have taken the following forms.

Money for industry. As we have already seen investment in industry has been much lower in Britain than in other advanced capitalist countries. This has arisen because of the

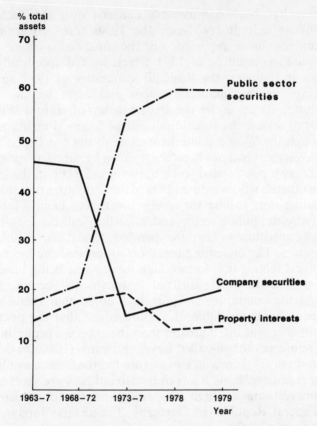

FIGURE 3.7 *Insurance companies' investments*

SOURCE: Derived from data in Wilson Report (1980) *Committee to Review the Functioning of Financial Institutions*, Cmnd 7939 (London: HMSO).

low profits to be made in British industry, particularly in the traditional industries facing lack of demand and increased competition from abroad. Banks, pension funds, insurance companies have all limited their investment and lending in the industrial sector. Figure 3.7 shows the fall-off in the purchase of company securities by insurance companies from the early 1970s onwards. Indeed, the financial institutions have been remarkably successful in channelling the funds of declining companies to more profitable sectors.

There has been considerable concern over this lack of investment in industry. Since the 1930s three government committees have reported on the financial system: the Macmillan committee of 1931 which looked specifically at finance in industry, the Radcliffe committee of 1959 on the workings of the financial system and more recently the committee set up under the chairmanship of Harold Wilson (1980) to review the functioning of the financial institutions. Although the Wilson committee came to the conclusion that real investment had not been constrained by supply of external finance, two points need to be borne in mind. First, the trade union officials who were members of the committee presented a dissenting note calling for a new investment facility funded jointly by the public sector and what they call the long-term funding institutions, i.e. the pension funds and insurance companies. The dissenting members articulated the feeling of organised labour that not enough money was being invested into productive and industrial employment. Second, even though the committee's report had noted that there were sufficient funds available, it acknowledged that the price of such finance was often greater than the expected profitability. This reinforces the so-called Lever–Edwards (1980a,b) thesis, that not only is there a lack of finance but the finance available is too expensive. Bank loans to British industry are short-term and interest rates are high compared to finance for industry in the Federal Republic of Germany, France and Japan. The consequence is that industry is hamstrung by the need to depend on expensive borrowing just to survive, let alone embark on an ambitious programme of real investment. Because bank lending to industry has been low and prohibitively expensive there has been a downward spiral of lack of investment – low productivity –lack of competitiveness – few orders – and back to low investments through high unemployment. The net effect is for a slow process of deindustrialisation speeded up during world slumps.

Although in international terms the record of investment has been low, there has been some institutional involvement in the industrial sector. The big institutions have been increasing their share in equity markets. In 1957 financial institutions held 21 per cent of UK ordinary shares but by 1978 this had soared to 50 per cent. However, investment has been into the major, safe companies while small firms and those involved in speculative enterprises often find it difficult to get loans or attract investment. The big institutions are conservative; what they want is high, safe and secure returns on their investment. Chances have been taken in the industrial sector but for the most part there has been a policy of backing known winners. Investment analysts often make a distinction between the lagging 'sunset' industries which fail to attract much investment and the booming 'sunrise' industries where high profits can be made. A typical example of a sunrise industry is electronics and a typical firm is Micro Consultants Ltd. This company was established in 1967 in Newbury, Berkshire. It now employs 400 people, a third of whom have university degrees, compared with only 6 per cent of the national workforce. The firm has two sites, one in Newbury consisting of four half-timbered cottages, and the other a large country house in Kenley, Surrey. The firm produces computer-based equipment such as the machine which allows multi-split screen images to be shown on television at varying speeds. The company is valued at £100 million on the Stock Exchange and in the past five years profits have grown by 466 per cent. Micro Consultants Ltd is an important exemplar case. It has a number of characteristics which are found throughout the expanding sunrise sectors. It employs few people and is not tied to traditional industrial premises. Unlike the older declining industries it is not bound to specific locations because of raw material or transport requirements. It is the supply of skilled labour which is of prime importance. There is a concentration of sunrise industries in the South-East, as firms swarm around the expanding M4 corridor from West London through Bracknell to Reading, Newbury and Bristol, although in the North-West and Scotland, many of the routine production line processes are carried out. This too exemplifies the general case. There is a tendency in high-technology industries for the research and development sites to be located in the South-East while the basic production is carried out in the peripheral regions. Since the sunrise industries require only a small workforce they will do little to mop up the huge pool of unemployed, semi-skilled and even skilled workers.

If investment in industry has been low and guided towards safe, secure companies which add little to the employment prospects of unskilled school-leavers, where has all the institutional money been going?

Property. Institutional involvement in property is enormous. And it has been growing. There has been a 460 per cent increase in real terms in the last twenty years. Money going into property has taken two main forms:

(1) There has been lending and, more important latterly, investment by the banks, pension funds and insurance companies in commercial and industrial property and agricultural land-holdings.
(2) There has been the lending of money for the purchase of houses by individual households. This mortgage business is dominated by the building societies and, more recently, the banks.

(1) Institutions have always been attracted to commercial and industrial property because of its fixed supply. Given the absolute qualities of prime urban sites and the operation of the land use planning system which limits the amount of land available for commercial development, scarcity has been assured. And where there is scarcity there are rising values. Property investment has the potential to provide long-term high yields. Moreover, commercial property is a commodity which is relatively trouble-free. It is easier to value than, say, new firms and investors do not need to do much apart from reassessing rents once a client has been found.

Institutional involvement in property in post-war Britain began in the first property boom after the abolition of building licences in 1954. It took the form of lending money to property developers. The replacement of central city properties was a hugely lucrative enterprise and the institutions eventually sought to acquire equity interests. When the second property boom took off in the late 1960s the institutions moved into property in a big way. In 1974 just over 20 per cent of the total investment of pension funds and insurance companies was flowing into the property sector. Property, an undemanding commodity with relatively easy appraisal with a prospect of both rapid short-term gain and long-term steady yield, was an attractive investment for the big institutions seeking to find a profitable home for their funds. However, the property boom peaked in 1974 and by the end of 1975 and throughout 1976 property yields declined. And ever-mindful of relative rates of return, the relative proportion of institutional investment declined to between 12 and 13 per cent by 1979. The absolute amount, however, increased as the falling proportion was counterbalanced by the huge absolute increase in institutional funds. The property assets of pension funds and insurance companies increased from £128 million in 1965 to £17,079 million in 1979. This huge flow has been one of the main lubricants of property speculation and commercial redevelopment of Britain's inner city areas. The consequences for local communities of this mass of investment in the built environment will be discussed in Chapter 5. The 1970s also saw growing institutional investment in the rural land market (Munton, 1977), the scale of which prompted a government report (Northfield Report, 1979).

(2) The mass of institutional involvement in the property market has been in the form of lending for house purchase finance. The largest single set of institutions in this market are the building societies. Over 80 per cent of building society funds are devoted to mortgages and they are currently lending over £6,000 million each year. They have provided between 70 to 98 per cent of all mortgages throughout the 1970s. The societies operate by attracting savings. Their inflow of funds is dependent upon the relative rates of interest offered. When banks offer better rates, money flows from the building society into the banks. As the amount of personal savings has increased and building societies provided relatively good rates of return, so their share of personal savings has increased from 16 per cent in 1966 to 28 per cent in 1978. Building societies are now the third largest financial institution in the country after banks and insurance companies.

The growth of the building societies reflects their competitive position in the personal savings market, a position guaranteed by successive governments eager to encourage owner-occupation. On the supply side the state has given a privileged position to building societies; they were not subject to restrictions on reserve: asset ratios or 'corset' restrictions made on the banks. Government aid even extended to three-month bridging loans when funds dried up. On the demand side the state has made owner-occupation fiscally desirable with income tax relief on mortgage interest repayments and the profits on the sale of houses not being subject to capital gains tax. The tax system has so structured the tenure choice that most people now prefer owner-occupation.

Building societies have to secure members' deposits. Translated into mortgage lending this appears as a policy of risk minimisation. Building societies prefer to lend to young people on salaries purchasing standard properties (semi-detached or detached dwellings) in wholly residential areas. They do not offer such favourable payment terms for non-standard properties or for the purchase of dwellings in certain inner city areas. The explicit discrimination against inner city areas has been termed 'red-lining'. There is a large and growing body of evidence which points to its existence in contemporary British cities (Short, 1982b).

Mortgage lending has been a lucrative business for the building societies. With a huge demand created by government policies, building societies have been able to pick and choose customers. But the attractions of the mortgage business have caught the attention of the banks whose share of mortgage lending has increased from 2 per cent in 1976 to almost 20 per cent in 1981. For them, lending in the property market is simply more profitable than lending to British industry.

Bridging the government's fiscal gap. The growing fiscal imbalance between public expenditure and revenue has introduced a new investment opportunity for the investing institutions. Public sector securities as a proportion of their total assets have increased throughout the 1970s and are now the main destination of institutional investment.

Because public expenditure has been outrunning revenue the government has sought to bridge the fiscal gap by borrowing. This takes a number of forms. In the fiscal year 1980–1, for example, direct borrowing by local government and public corporations amounted to £1,237 million and £372 million respectively, the national saving schemes brought in £2,162 million, and the sale of British government securities (gilts) provided a massive £13,083 million. The sale of gilts is the main way in which the government finances expenditure and this market is dominated by the investing institutions. They have been encouraged to purchase gilts because of the high rates of return and the increasingly monetarist persuasion of successive governments in the 1970s. An important aim of monetarist policies is control of the money supply and, since the main increase in money supply come from bank lending, one way to control it is to reduce government dependence on banks. Borrowing from non-banking institutions such as the insurance companies and pension funds through the sale of gilt-edged stocks thus becomes of prime importance. But the institutions will only purchase such stock if the yield is high and the government can only sell its stock when interest rates are high. The power of the institutions to secure high returns was amply demonstrated during 1976 when they refused to buy gilts until the Bank of England's minimum lending rate was pushed up two points. The 'gilt strike' was effective.

Through the institutions the government is able to finance expenditure. But at a price. Interest rates are kept high, which works against manufacturing industry and households with mortgages, while debt interests crowd out other forms of public expenditure. In 1981–2 debt interest amounted to £12,800 million out of a total expenditure of £117,000 million, more than three times that payed to the unemployed, more than twice that spent on housing and only slightly less than the total amount spent on the National Health Service (NHS).

Investing overseas. For most of the post-war period the financial institutions have been inhibited from investing overseas because of exchange controls exercised by the government since 1947. Overseas portfolio investment had to be financed with currency bought directly on the international money market or against the collateral of securities at specified rates. The net effect was to limit the amount of investment overseas. But the exchange controls were abolished by the Conservative government in October 1979. The effect was marked. Table 3.3 shows the increase in acquisition of overseas assets and Figure 3.8 shows how the portfolio investments of the financial

TABLE 3.3 *Acquisition of overseas assets by financial institutions*

	Acquisition overseas (£ m)		
	1978	1979	1980
Investment and unit trusts	17	334	603
Pension funds	372	384	1186
Insurance companies	—	221	689

SOURCE: Treasury (1981a) 'Ending Exchange Controls', Economic Progress Report No. 138, table 2.

institutions increased, helping to boost the net overseas capital flow from Britain. The institutions are increasing the overseas part of their portfolios as a response to the more attractive yields compared to British company securities. One favoured investment has been property and there has been a growing interest in the US property market as relative yields in Britain's property interests have declined. The pension funds launched a British American Property Unit Trust in 1982 to channel investment into office building, shopping centres and industrial parks in North America. At its launch the trust had already secured nearly £28 million worth of funds.

The flow of investment overseas is just one response to the changing balance of relative rates of return and yields afforded by the investment opportunities available to the investing institutions. New investment flows into those sectors yielding the highest returns. In the early 1970s property was providing higher yields in company securities but by the late 1970s government securities were a more profitable investment and after 1979, with the lifting of exchange controls, lucrative overseas opportunities beckoned the hot money of the institutions.

Conclusions

In summary, the response of capital to the crisis of the British economy has been:

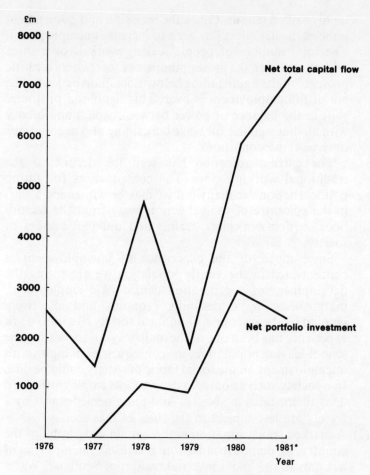

FIGURE 3.8 *Overseas investment*

* First half.

SOURCE: Derived from data in Treasury (1981a) 'Ending Exchange Controls', Economic Progress Report No. 138.

(1) Not to invest in manufacturing industry but to direct investment overseas into property and government securities where higher, safer returns are available. Some British investment has been made but mainly in the high-technology industries which require only small amounts of

highly skilled labour. Given the recession and government policies the net effect has been to increase unemployment. The total number of people seeking work is over three million and even the most optimistic of forecasters see little prospect of the figure falling below 1.5 million by 1990. The era of full employment is over. This signifies a profound shift in the balance of power between capital and labour with all that signifies for wage bargaining and negotiations over working conditions.

The current recession has seen the decline of the traditional working class. The consequences for future political action are many but we may be witnessing a shift in the epicentre of radical action away from the factory floor to non-workplace realms and different sectors of society.

Since much of the experience of unemployment is concentrated in the youth population we are seeing the development of a generation denied paid employment, marginalised by a declining economy and effectively ignored by the discourse of political society. Because work experience has been one of the main ways of socialising the school-leaving population, the consequences of high youth unemployment on the social fabric of society could be dire. In a society such as ours, to deny people employment is to deny them status in society. And those denied status by a society are less subject to the rules of that society.

(2) A marked transformation in the human geography of the country as deindustrialisation increased unemployment not only in the 'old' industrial regions of Scotland, Wales and the North but also in the regions with 'new' industries such as the Midlands. The country is divided in economic experience at the regional level between the affluent parts of the South-East and East Anglia where 'sunrise' industries are being established and the other regions where 'sunset' industries predominate. Government policies which put emphasis on controlling inflation rather than reducing unemployment have marked regional consequences as they lead to worsening of regional employment inequalities. The Thatcher government was and is the government for and of the affluent regions. At the subregional level the

manufacturing sectors of urban economies have declined most. What little net growth there has been is concentrated in the small towns and rural areas of the 'sunbelt'. Those trapped in the city have been stranded by the ebbing economic tide.

(3) More generally there has been what Miller (1978) has described as the 'recapitalisation of capital'. This involves cuts in welfare expenditure and a redirecting of government policies and expenditures towards the private sector. There has been a recommodification of many public goods and services (see Harloe, 1981 for a discussion of housing) switched from non-market mechanisms of allocation to provision by market or quasi-market forces. Recent policies and political debates have signalled a weakening of welfarism, the promotion of individualism and the creation of a more unequal society.

The debates and the policies have been very largely contested in, through and against the state. It is to an examination of this arena within an arena that we now turn.

4
The State: Arena within an Arena

A major actor in the urban arena is the state. Throughout the post-war period its size and level of intervention in Britain has been growing. In managing the economy, framing laws, taxing and spending, the state affects all areas of our lives. It is a major factor in contemporary society.

The state is not one single actor and its actions cannot be seen as uni-causal or uni-directional. There is the government, the body of elected representatives at both the central and local level and there is the apparatus of the state manned by non-elected officials again at both the national and local levels. To assume harmony is to ignore the tension between members and officers, central and local government and the different parts of the state apparatus.

The machinery of the British state is driven by two impulses. The first comes from the need to maintain mass social allegiance and reflect popular opinion. The political parties express public opinion in order to achieve electoral success. In a democracy, popular appeal is a prerequisite for electoral victory. That is why manifestos and party political arguments appeal implicitly and explicitly to the 'national' or 'general interest'; the terms cover the majority of voters. The inability of individual parties to achieve electoral success is political failure, a crisis for the party and its supporters; the failure of the whole system to maintain political credibility is a crisis of legitimation. Expression of public political opinion through the political process is mediated by party ideology which is as much a function of the past as an indication of the present. Contemporary political debates echo loudly with the argument and the experience of the past. Parties are also influenced by pressure groups. Electors are consulted irregularly and are asked to record one vote, to express one preference from the variety of parties each offering a range of policies. The relationship between electors and policy outputs is tenuous. Much more direct is the relationship between government and pressure groups expressing specific interests. There are of course pressure groups and pressure groups. The CBI and the Trades Union Congress (TUC) have more muscle and more direct access to government than, say, the Women's Institute, while Wimpey and Bovis construction companies have a more direct line to the Department of the Environment than Lower Earley Resident's Association. The term 'imperfect pluralism' has been coined to refer to the existence of many groups with differential access to the levers of power. In the major issues such as management of the economy, the big pressure groups dominate. Middlemas (1979) has suggested that the history of twentieth-century politics in Britain – at least from 1911 until the mid 1960s – has been one of consensus between the corporate triangle of government, unions and employers, as each recognised the need for compromise with the others.

The second has come from the economic pressure of a capitalist market, and a declining one at that. The state is called upon in a capitalist society to secure and maintain the position of capital both in relation to labour and in relation to foreign capital. These demands are expressed through pressure groups and the economic reality of a capitalist system. In an expanding economy there is no great tension between the two impulses. A booming economy means the position of capital is assured and there is enough public money to provide the range of public goods and services which allow increases in private affluence and maintain mass integration and social allegiance. There is no crisis of legitimation, as the context which allows capital accumulation also maintains political allegiance and social peace. This was the state of affairs in post-war Britain up until the mid 1960s. In this period the bargain between capital and labour was struck, with the state called upon to ensure full employment and provide for a welfare society. The bargain held because the growth in the world economy allowed British goods to be sold abroad despite the relative lack of competition while imports were limited. The ending of the world boom became the British slump as import penetration increased and export performance declined. The constants of full employment and rising expectations began to disappear as their continued existence was no longer possible without massive state spending with the consequent potential and reality for inflation. The compromise between the corporate triangle was beginning to disappear as unemployment rose and welfare expenditure was reduced. State expenditures could no longer keep both capital and labour happy while union bosses could no longer control their members if rising living standards were not assured and, in the increasingly competitive world market, employers were asking for new means to strengthen their hand against organised labour. In an economically declining capitalist democracy the tension between the two impulses becomes apparent as the pressures of the markets strain against the political realities of a discontented electorate. The state is the arena for this tension.

The logic of capital is strongest in the Treasury and central government while the political arguments are more apparent with elected representatives, local government and the central government spending departments. The running battles between the Labour party and the Treasury, between central and local governments, between representatives and officers, between spending departments and Right-wing politicians, between Left-wing politicians and the Treasury all reflect these basic tensions. Saunders (1980) has characterised central–local relations, for example, in the following manner:

> We must distinguish between social investment policies determined within the corporate sector at national and regional levels of government, and social consumption policies, determined through competitive political struggles often at local level. This means that the tension between economic and social priorities, between rational planning and democratic accountability and between centralised direction and local responsiveness tend to underlie one another. (p. 551)

Britain is not alone in facing these problems. The work of Habermas (1976) in Germany and that of O'Connor (1973) in the United States point to similar sorts of tensions. But in

Britain the rate of economic decline has been faster and more precipitous than other advanced capitalist countries.

The emerging tensions were outlined in Figure 2.5 as a series of possible crises. The use of the term 'crisis' does not imply an apocalyptic breakdown. Rather it signifies a profound change whose future direction is uncertain and whose outcome will have marked redistributional consequences. In Chinese the word for crisis is composed of two figures. One signifies danger, the other opportunity. The term crisis is used with this ambivalent quality in mind. The dangers to some are the opportunities of others. Four possible crises were outlined. The state's economic role (rationality crisis type 1 in Figure 2.5) has already been discussed in Chapters 2 and 3. In this chapter we will examine in more detail the possibilities, articulation and resolution of legitimation crisis, fiscal crisis and rationality crises.

The politics of economic decline

The perceived reality of economic decline has had a profound effect on the British political scene. For the period 1964–76 James Alt has shown how, even though individual well-being increased, the majority of people were acutely aware of how national economic performance, measured by such things as unemployment, inflation and strikes, declined. The result was a feeling that governments could do little to halt the process. Successive governments had promised but failed to deliver. Over the period there was a sustained decline in instrumental voting as people saw little effective government action in halting the seemingly inexorable economic decay. Individual improvement was represented as a function of self-motivation, luck and hard work while national decline was a function of government incompetence. As Alt (1979, p. 269) notes:

In large measure, then, the story of the mid-1970s is the story of a politics of declining expectations . . . not a politics of protest, but a politics of quiet disillusion, a politics in which lack of involvement or indifference to organised party politics was the most important feature.

This indifference has been registered in the decline of Britain's two-party system. In 1964, 40 per cent of the electorate said they were either 'very strong' or 'fairly strong' supporters of one of the two main parties but by 1979 this figure has fallen to 20 per cent. Electoral turn-out in national elections has also decreased; from over 80 per cent in the 1950s to just over 75 per cent in the 1980s while electoral turn-out at local elections regularly fails to encompass more than 40 per cent of the electorate. Figure 4.1 shows the reduction in voting for the two major parties since 1955, high point of the post-war consensus. Each party has its own specific reasons for loss of electoral support. These are undoubtedly complex, but in general one can say that the Conservatives have lost the label and the record of the natural party of government as their policies have come to be seen by many as socially divisive, while Labour's decline is due to the unpopularity of their main policies of nationalisation, their perceived association with high taxation and to their strong ties with the union movement. Their

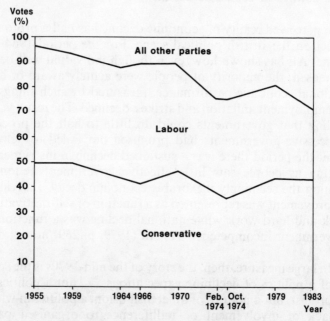

FIGURE 4.1   *Voting in post-war elections*

traditional manual working-class base has also been eroded by changes in occupational composition. The loosening of the two-party system as a whole is a more general function of Britain's economic decline. Successive governments have sought to alleviate the problem but, since many of the putative solutions involve major cuts in welfare expenditure and reductions in individual well-being for the mass of workers, they have been caught between the pincers of economic reality and political realism. It is only a recent phenomenon to promise a hair shirt rather than a bed of roses.

Since the management of the economy has become the main criterion on which electors judge governments, governments have acted accordingly. Throughout the 1950s and early 1960s successive Conservative governments, for example, manipulated demand management in order to coincide with elections. Well before an election there would be sufficient pump-priming to boost demand, wages and consumer expenditure. The political–business cycle operated to maximise the political advantage and electoral chances of the party in power (Stewart, 1978). Indeed this explicit manipulation of consumer demand in order to win elections has been cited as one of the main reasons behind Britain's rapid post-war decline (see Brittan, 1964). In any event there is a clear temporal rhythm to economic policy, marching to the beat of the electoral drum. Parties win power by appealing to electors.

Between the electoral victory and the implementation of policy falls the shadow of economic reality. Individuals have votes but capital has power. Although electoral politics decide who is in government, elections are not 'about "who governs" but about who chairs the meetings at which those with power and authority try to reach agreement' (Alderman, 1978, 207). The potency of mass political representation is further limited in the British system of government through three other factors:

(1) *Government controls of parliament*. Through its control of the voting majority in the House of Commons (through party discipline and the adversary political system), parliamentary time, generation of legislation and information, the government – and more particularly the Cabinet –

blunts the power of elected representatives and democratic debate. As Cabinet rather than parliament becomes the main power centre so closed discussion replaces democratic debate and a closed order dominates over an open system of government: trends made easier and more pronounced by economic decline with its consequent promotion of pragmatism over political values and the lauding of 'reality' over 'ideology'.

(2) *Growth of 'quangos'.* In post-war Britain there has been an enormous growth of independent bodies which perform public functions outside the parliamentary system, sometimes known as 'quangos' (quasi-autonomous non-government organisations). There are almost 2,000 quangos (outside nationalised industries and the NHS) which together spent £6,000 million and employed 25,000 full-time people in 1980–1. Much of this growth can be seen as part of the spawning of quasi-state institutions in order to cope with mounting levels of intervention. However, this growth also reflects the administrative means to short-circuit other public organisations and forums considered unreliable and untrustworthy. The growth of quangos is more than just a form of creeping bureaucracy, then, it is a bypass around the free flow of democratic traffic. Staffed by the worthies drawn from the list of the great and the good, quangos can, in theory at least, be relied upon to provide 'impartial' advice and 'sensible' action. The inverted commas indicate that the definitions of these terms are not innocent. Although the Conservative government was committed to cutting the size of powerful quangos, the cuts which it introduced in 1980 were not only cosmetic, coming up as they did against entrenched positions, but directed (Hood, 1981). Thus, the Centre for Environmental Studies, the Central Health Services Council and the Personal Social Services Council, all of which provided potential platforms for articulated protest against government policy, were axed. At the same time the government set up the Urban Development Corporations to provide incentives to private capital, in Merseyside and London docklands. It would seem that it is not quangos *per se* that are wrong but politically unreliable quangos.

(3) *Bureaucratic power*. Britain's government is served by a full-time, non-partisan civil service. In its sheer professionalism the British civil service has much to recommend it and is generally regarded as both competent and good. However, a great deal of power is concentrated at the very senior levels. The civil servants are certainly civil; the question is how servile. With their longer term in departments than ministers, senior officials have more information, and more departmental knowledge than their succession of often transient political masters. The power of the civil service haunts both parties. Radical Conservatives see their market philosophy as being undermined by the Keynesian beliefs of senior civil servants, while Labour supporters see their socialism betrayed by a civil service establishment. In a sense both are partly right. The senior central government civil service is a service dominated by the tenets of the post-war boom, with a belief in the mixed economy and a commitment to the welfare state being the principle features. The current mandarins are less happy with extremes of either right or left. The 1979 Conservative government marked the political beginning of radical post-war governments and perhaps the beginning of new tensions between senior government ministers and the senior officials of the big spending departments.

In politics as in physics some of Newton's laws seem to hold. To every action there is a political reaction. Thus although the politics of closed discussion has closed off public debate, there have been political counter-trends. Since 1979, for example, Select Committees of the House of Commons have been established and these have the power to examine ministers and senior civil servants alike. The politically vigorous backbenchers now have a forum to exercise their virility. Since their establishment these committees and their reports have provided a counter-weight to bland government pronouncement. In a real if limited sense the committees extend the scope of our political comment. Within some of the political parties the same thing is happening. The attempt to democratise the Labour party, for example, is an attempt to give greater power to the rank and file and less to the MPs who, it has been argued, are more liable to be sucked into corporate compromises. Moreover quangos, like royal commissions and committees of enquiry, do not necessarily complement the government of the day. The Manpower Services Commission, for instance has long been a loud and frequent critic of government employment policies. Ultimately, of course, governments can ignore reports and disband quangos – likely events when the level of popular pressure is low or not effectively mobilised.

These counter-trends are important. But they would seem to be a reaction. The main trend, the dominant political action of a Britain in decline, is towards a less democratic, more closed society. The politics of economic decline are the politics of conflict and governments find compromise in controlled agendas, selected priorities and rehearsed arguments in rooms closed to all but the quiet voices of 'reason' and 'moderation'.

But people have votes. We have already seen that the support for the traditional parties has been declining. There has also been a change in the geography of representation. In his examination of British elections from 1966 to 1979, Taylor (1979) noted a marked polarisation in voting patterns. The data in Table 4.1 and Figure 4.2 indicate the nature of the

TABLE 4.1 *Swings to Conservative, 1966–79*

Region	Swing	Region	Swing
1. Strathclyde	−2·2	13. West Midlands Conurbation	5·9
2. East-Central Scotland	−0·2	14. Rest of West Midlands	9·9
3. Rural Scotland	3·7	15. East Midlands	10·6
4. Rural North	8·4	16. East Anglia	9·5
5. Industrial North-East	3·3	17. Devon and Cornwall	14·0
6. Merseyside	3·4	18. Rest of South West	12·8
7. Greater Manchester	4·4	19. Inner London	6·0
8. Rest of North West	8·2	20. Outer London	8·9
9. West Yorkshire	5·3	21. Outer Metropolitan Area	14·5
10. South Yorkshire	5·7	22. Outer South East	12·1
11. Rural Wales	13·3		
12. Industrial Wales	6·6	Great Britain	7·6

* Swing calculated as the change in the Conservative percentage of the total vote for Conservative and Labour.

SOURCE: Taylor, P. J. (1979) 'The Changing Geography of Representation in Britain', *Area*, vol. 11, pp. 289–94.

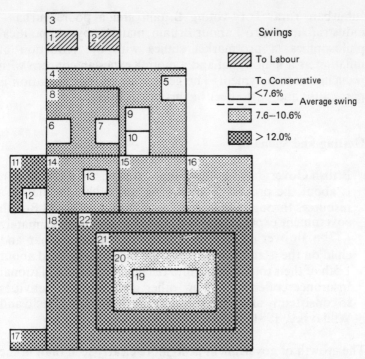

Swings

////// To Labour

To Conservative

☐ <7.6%

— — — — — — Average swing

7.6–10.6%

▓▓ > 12.0%

FIGURE 4.2 *The geography of voting swings, 1966–79**

* See Table 4.1 for numbered regions.

SOURCE: Taylor (1979).

change, a shift 'which has left the urban industrial regions relatively more pro-Labour existing in a sea of increasing Conservative support' (Taylor, 1979, p. 291). In the 1979 election Thatcherland was the prosperous South-East of England and rural and suburban areas in other regions.

This pattern of support had an important implication. During the early 1980s as unemployment increased in the peripheral regions and urban centres the party of government drew its support and its information from the least affected areas of the country. Tory Cabinet ministers represented those parts of the country the recession was affecting least. The uneven patterns of economic decline are reflected in political representation. If this pattern of polarisation continues we will see the re-emergence of the two nations, a relatively rich suburban–rural Tory-voting Britain and a poorer urban–industrial, more pro-Labour Britain, matched by two political philosophies, a pro-market stance with the reduction of inflation as a major goal and a more Keynesian concern with reducing unemployment. The geography of representation is part cause and part effect of this polarisation.

Getting and spending

> British Government is about many things, but if anything it is about the process of allocating up to half the nation's resources through public spending. During 1979–80 British government expenditures were estimated at approximately £87bn, or over £1,500 per year for every man, woman and child on the island. To help pay the bill, Britons paid about 1/5th of their total income into the income tax and National Insurance coffers . . . . Few other governmental activities so consistently affect the everyday life of citizens. (Heclo and Wildavsky, 1981, p. lxi)

The growth of government is no more clearly seen than in the realm of taxation and public expenditure. In post-war Britain taxation has widened and deepened while public expenditure has grown and multiplied (see Figure 4.3). In 1959 public expenditure was 33 per cent of GDP; by 1980 this figure had increased to 42 per cent. The biggest spender in contemporary Britain is government.

Much of the increased expenditure is in the form of spending on health, education, housing and social security. The growth of social spending has been part of the social-democratic compromise struck between capital and labour and between successive governments and the electorate in the post-war years. More hospitals, better social insurance and increased educational opportunities were all part of the tide of post-war rising expectations. But as the economy faltered, problems arose. On the revenue-raising side, firms wanted taxation to be reduced in order to reduce their own losses, while there were sharp political limits to the taxation of private individuals. On the revenue spending side, there were increased costs and more

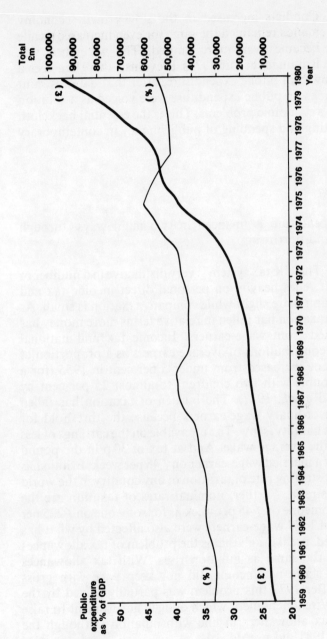

FIGURE 4.3   *The rise of public expenditure in the United Kingdom*

* At current prices.

SOURCE: *Economic Trends.*

demands. Conflicts increased in the slow-growth economy because demands remained the same (or even increased) while resources became even more limited. The watershed was reached in Britain in the mid 1970s. Previously there had been a steady growth in public expenditure; after that date restraint and cutbacks on public expenditure were voiced as a solution to Britain's economic problems. This is the essential backcloth to the getting and spending of public money in contemporary Britain.

The getting

Public expenditure is financed in two main ways, through taxation and borrowing.

Taxation. The UK tax system is very distinctive in a number of respects. It relies heavily on personal direct income tax and taxes on capital are slight while company taxation is small. As company taxation has fallen in relative terms more money has been needed from wage-earners. Income tax and national insurance contributions of average earners as a proportion of gross income increased from under 5 per cent in 1955 (for a married couple with two children) to almost 25 per cent by 1975 (Field *et al.*, 1977). The burden of taxation has fallen mainly on ordinary wage-earners because the threshold for income tax liability is low. Tax is payable on the earnings of less than half the average wage. And at tax of 30 p in the pound payable by a married wage-earner on £45 per week, Britain has the highest starting rate of taxation of any country in the world except Australia. Further, nominal rates of taxation are the same for someone on £45 per week as for someone on £225 per week. Until 1977 wage-earners were also affected by what has been termed 'fiscal drag': that is the problem of tax allowances remaining the same as inflation rises. With tax allowances remaining static net income did not keep pace with gross income. After 1977 this problem was partially solved by the Rooker–Wise amendment which obliged government to raise personal tax allowances in line with inflation (although the budget of 1981 did not do so).

There are two traps in the tax system for the low wage-earner. In the *poverty trap* low wage-earners gain nothing or even lose from an earnings increase because it results in more taxation and loss of entitlements. A couple with two children with a gross income of £50 per week receive a net income of £95.87 through family income supplement and other benefits. The same family earning £100 per week gross lose benefits and have a net income of £93.50. In the *unemployment trap* low wage-earners find it more financially rewarding to be out of work. The self-same couple earning £100 per week gross will receive £93.50 net after tax and national insurance have been paid. With unemployment benefit the net weekly sum is £83.80. After allowing for the costs of work (travelling, clothes, etc.,) the benefits of paid employment are less than marginal. In 1980 almost five and a half million people, 20 per cent of the labour force, were affected by these 'traps', although the unemployment trap is diminishing in importance because of reductions in unemployment benefit.

In essence the expansion of the welfare state through increased public expenditure was paid for primarily by the mass of ordinary wage-earners. The welfare state became the poor man's burden as much as the refuge of the needy. The social welfare system was paid for by the working class and involved the redistribution of income not from the rich to the poor but from young, healthy wage-earners to the old, sick and disabled and unemployed. Those most likely to benefit from the truly redistributional social welfare have in Britain paid for the system. This has a number of implications. It has meant a wide and deep tax base. Any political party that promotes tax cuts may not win an election but it is half-way there. One of the reasons behind Labour's electoral decline has been their failure to address the problem of restructuring the British taxation system. Too many socialists have simply assumed that greater equality comes from greater public spending without looking at the financing of this expenditure.

Borrowing. Governments unlike private individuals and companies with stingy bank managers spend more than they take in receipts. They bridge this fiscal gap by borrowing. The Public Sector Borrowing Requirement (PSBR) is the difference between government expenditure and government receipts. There has been a fluctuating long-term increase in the PSBR with a marked increase in the mid 1970s when public expenditure rose dramatically because of a mixture of successful wage claims by public sector unions, general price inflation and overestimation of rates of economic growth; all these combined to open the chasm between what the government took in and what it was spending. The PSBR bridged the gap. The rise of the PSBR played an important part in the new post-Keynesian economics. If Keynesianism was the official economics of the boom, then monetarism became the official line for its fiscal aftermath. Its central principle was a belief in the need to control and reduce government spending and borrowing. Too much spending and borrowing, it was argued, created high inflation rates and crowded out private investment. Given the constraints on government's ability to increase receipts the need to limit borrowing obviously implied the need to reduce spending. The Conservative government which came to power in 1979 aimed to reduce the PSBR through a combination of using North Sea Oil receipts and reducing public expenditure programmes.

The spending

Two broad periods of government spending in post-war Britain can be identified. First, there is the period of growth between the early 1950s and the mid 1970s when total public expenditure increased by over 150 per cent. Much of this increased expenditure went into what may be termed social expenditure, involving spending on education, health, housing, social services and employment. The largest increases were in these social spending categories. In 1951 defence expenditure took up just over a quarter of total public expenditure while social expenditure took 44 per cent. By 1981 defence spending constituted 10 per cent and social expenditure 55 per cent. By 1981 defence spending constituted 10 per cent and social expenditure 55 per cent. In a real expenditure sense Britain changed in the post-war years from a WARFARE–welfare state to a WELFARE–warfare state.

The commitment to full employment and widespread provision of welfare facilities meant growing expenditure as the state became the main provider of a whole set of goods and services ranging from six-lane motorways to grants for industrialists setting up in peripheral regions. The price of social peace was social welfare programmes and the use of public expenditure to mop up unemployment. The specific factors behind the growth of expenditure were need, rising expectations, the ballot box and inflation. Once the system was established, demographic changes prompted greater use of its resources. In the 1950s and 1960s there was the baby boom, then in the 1970s the growth of the gerontocracy. These demographic changes created a potential need which was turned into demand by the rise of expectation. People began to call on and rely on the state much more. There was a subtle but nonetheless progressive shift in attitudes, as what had once been seen as 'welfare handouts' were increasingly seen as the exercise of one's rights. The professional groups involved also sought to attain higher standards of service provision. Teachers' unions, for example, lobbied for more resources, new schools and smaller classes. Politicians also got elected on the promise of giving something in return. The thirteen years of Tory rule from 1951 to 1964 saw the political use of the business cycle to an unprecedented extent. As we have seen, before an election the economy was primed in order to increase employment and consumer spending. Finally there was inflation, which directly increased the costs of everything the state did. In the sphere of social expenditure service costs were always higher (this is termed the 'relative price effect') because of the labour-intensive nature and their relatively lower labour productivity. Compared to other sectors, therefore, the costs of social services were increasing in relative terms each year even without an increase in services.

The specific form of expenditure varies by programme (see Figure 4.4). Over 90 per cent of expenditure in the social security programme, for example, is transfer payments of cash subsidies to households. In the health, education and law and order fields, in contrast, the biggest single expenditure is pay, and in the defence field the largest expenditure is the purchase of capital goods. We also have to identify the outputs and

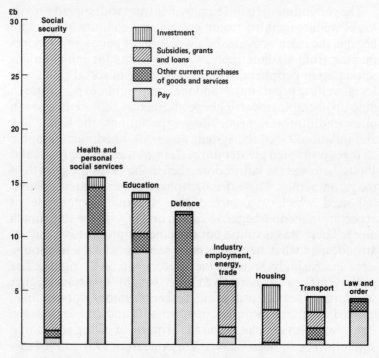

FIGURE 4.4 *Main public expenditure programmes, 1981–2*

SOURCE: Treasury (1982) *The Government's Expenditure Plans 1982–83 to 1984–85*, Cmnd 8494 (London: HMSO).

effects of all this government expenditure. O'Connor (1973) suggests that we can distinguish between social expenses expenditure (such as education) which maintains social harmony and social investment expenditures which help capital accumulation. In short, the idea is that we can distinguish between spending to meet popular demands and spending to increase and maintain profits. However this distinction is not an easy one to make. All spending on health may be seen as meeting popular demands for better welfare provision, but much of the expenditure goes to private contractors to build hospitals and to private drug companies to provide the necessary medicines. Health expenditures meet popular needs but they also give business to sections of capital. The difficulties are clear; we have to tease out public expenditure not only in terms of its aims but also its effects. Thus, while public expenditure in the health service was seen by its original architects as social expenses expenditure it is also the case that in a capitalist society private firms benefit; in this sense it is also social investment expenditure.

The creation of the welfare—warfare state has involved a dramatic improvement in the lives of ordinary people. The British population are now better housed, in better health and have greater educational opportunities than ever before. However, this new society has not involved a massive redistribution of wealth. The main beneficiaries of the expanded range of public goods and services have not been the poorest and weakest, but rather the middle-income groups whose sharp elbows assured them a high place in the distributional welfare benefits. In Britain many welfare benefits are not means-tested. Benefits accrue to those who are eligible and apply. The middle class have been the most adept at understanding and using the benefits system. Le Grand (1982) has examined the effects of government spending in a range of programmes from education and health through to housing. The inescapable conclusion is that the biggest recipients and the greatest gainers are the middle-income groups who receive tax relief on their mortgages, send their children to university and have good access to medical facilities.

The second period of public expenditure in Britain was the era of restraint and cutback emerging out of the mid 1970s. This two-fold categorisation does not constitute a clean break. There had been a series of expenditure reductions prior to 1975 in response to recurring economic difficulties (especially balance-of-payments problems) and even after 1975 certain programmes were expanded. Indeed public expenditure continued to increase in absolute terms after 1975, although as a proportion of GDP it levelled off. These qualifications mean that the division marks a change of opinion, in which the concept of public expenditure itself changes. As government expenditure continued to increase during the 1970s but Britain's economic performance continued to worsen, monetarist doctrines which saw government expenditure not as a solution but as a cause of economic decline began to gain ground. They achieved purchase in influential British circles because of the widespread taxation load used to fund public expenditure. Most people paid taxes and thus there was a majority opinion in favour of at most tax cuts and at the least a slowing down in the rate of tax increases. As Walker (1982) has noted: 'the mid 1970s represented in some senses a watershed, the end of a long era of steady growth in public spending and its replacement, in the short-term at least by severe restraint' (p. 9).

In the mid 1970s an official view of government spending was emerging which saw the need to control and eventually reduce government spending in order to lighten tax loads and to divert resources to aiding industry and exports. This was echoed in government reports which bridged the chasm of political differences. Thus in 1977 a White Paper (Treasury, 1977) produced by a Labour government could note that the intention was:

... to make possible a shift of resources into industrial investment and exports; to restrain the increase in the burden of taxation which would otherwise have been necessary; to maintain an appropriate balance between take-home pay and the provision of public services; and by these means to reduce inflationary pressure in the economy,

while three years later under a Conservative government another White Paper (Treasury, 1980) could note:

The Government intend to reduce public expenditure progressively in volume terms over the next four years . . . to bring down the rate of inflation and interest rates by controlling the growth of the money supply and controlling government borrowing; to restore incentives; and plan for spending which is comparable both with the objectives for taxation and borrowing and with the realistic assessment for the prospects of economic growth.

Attempts at restraining public expenditure were not new. In 1960 a committee was set up by the Chancellor of the Exchequer to inquire into the control of public expenditure. The Plowden committee reported in 1960 and from its recommendations was born the Public Expenditure Survey Committee (PESC) system. In essence, this system was a mechanism to plan public expenditure on a five-year rolling cycle. Expenditure was planned in terms of functional programmes, such as education, rather than spending authorities and in the form of constant prices not current prices. That is, expenditure was planned in terms of number of teachers, university places, etc. rather than in simple cost measures. Under PESC, Treasury officials scrutinised the spending programmes of the different departments and compared them with their assessment of economic performance. The proposals for future spending in the light of what the country could afford were then submitted to the Cabinet where some horse-trading was done especially between the ministers of the major spending departments. Althogh the PESC system was supposed to control public spending, it failed. Planning in volume terms meant an open-ended commitment to programmes even while costs spiralled. By 1974–5 it was felt that spending was getting out of control. The failure of PESC brought forth cash limits. These were introduced in 1976 to put limits on spending. There are now fiscal barriers to funding open-ended programmes and the departments wishing more money because of cost increases must make a new bid. As Wright (1981, p. 82), notes:

Resource planning through five year public expenditure plans gave way to short term financial control through cash limits. Increasingly, governments began to treat the aggregate total of public spending as a 'residual' determined by stipulated target levels for government borrowing, which in turn reflected broader monetary strategies. Implicit in this approach was the abandonment of the use of public spending as an instrument of demand management.

The emphasis on cash rather than volume, cost rather than quality was further demonstrated in 1981 when it was announced by the Chancellor that in future annual reviews of expenditure would be conducted in cash terms. The new cash planning system allows cost increases to be more immediately noted. Finance is now to determine expenditure not expenditure finance.

The introduction of cash limits was successful. So successful that in 1978–9 underspending amounted to £2.5 billion. But in the new fiscal climate, 'overspending is strongly suppressed; underspending occurs mild rebuke' (Heclo and Wildavsky, 1982, p. 107).

The more direct control over expenditure in order to restrain and reduce public spending has a number of facets. It implies:

(1) A prioritisation of expenditure in order for some spending programmes to be cut while some are maintained and yet others increased.
(2) A control over local authority as well as central government spending.
(3) Restrictions on public sector pay awards.

Let us examine each in turn.

(1) *Restraining, cutting and choosing*

To reduce or even maintain public expenditure in a period when costs are rising involves choosing spending programmes to be restrained and cut back. The amount of reduction is guided by what the government gets, what it borrows and what it chooses to accept as sacrosanct.

There are limits within which a government operates. First, the expenditure cutbacks are limited by commitments. On the one hand there are the contractual and administrative commitments which make it difficult for governments completely to abolish programmes. There is an element of administrative inertia which makes it difficult to roll back the creeping tide of incrementalism. On the other hand there are electoral commitments. As we have seen the British taxation system casts a wide and deep net. A government committed to tax reductions is therefore assured of some measure of electoral success. It is one of the few truisms of social science that, holding everything else constant, few people enjoy paying taxes and given the choice most people want to see a reduction in their tax burden. Governments are thus restricted in the amount they can take in the form of tax receipts. There are also existing commitments in the form of tax allowances which any government in Britain would find it difficult to alter. Mortgage interest relief for example to owner-occupiers cost the excheque over £1,500 million in 1979–80 while the capital gains tax relief enjoyed by owner-occupiers who sell their property was approximately £2,000 million. These and other subsidies vital for continued electoral support reduce the area of fiscal manoeuvrability.

Second, there are limits to the state's ability to plan and implement public expenditure programmes. Public expenditure programmes are based on predictions on future levels of economic activity, employment levels, rates of inflation, etc. The state has limited ability to predict the future acurately. Another indisputable law of social science is that governments can and do get it wrong. We live in an imperfect world where even the most careful and most short-term of predictions can flounder on the uncertain contours of unfolding reality. The failure of the economy to match government's predictions has consistently upset expenditure plans.

To these general limits must be added the specific ones operating on any particular set by their position in economic time and the self-imposed constraints set by the ideological electoral baggage they take into office. Consider the case of the Conservative party which came into government in 1979 promising to reduce inflation. In order to reduce inflation they set themselves the target of holding expenditure constant for the year 1979–80 leading to reductions in later years and within this planned total reduction they aimed to spend more on defence and law and order. The reality was slightly different. The standstill was not achieved and spending increased 2 per cent between 1979–80 and 1980–1.

The main reason behind the disparity between plan and reality was the slump which increased unemployment and reduced the tax load. A Treasury report concluded that the recession had the following effects:

On expenditure
- more social security expenditure because of higher unemployment
- more redundancies meaning higher payments out of redundancy funds
- higher take-up of special employment measures

● larger loans to nationalised industries because of loss of sales caused by fall of demand in the economy
● earlier deliveries by private firms carrying out government contracts due to a fall in orders from the private sector. This reduced the shortfall in public expenditure.

On receipts
● lower receipt of income tax and national insurance contributions because of more unemployed and less overtime
● lower receipts from company taxes because of fallen profits
● lower receipts from expenditure taxes, such as VAT, because of a lower volume of sales.

It was estimated that the cost to the Exchequer, in terms of benefits payed out and taxes lost, of each unemployed person amounted to nearly £3,500 (Treasury, 1981b). In effect, the recession reduced the government's options as social security payments increased from 21 per cent of government expenditure in 1976–7 to 25 per cent in 1980–1 and 27 percent by 1981–2. The government's expenditure plans have not been completely achieved.

However there has been some reduction from previous government's commitments to the social welfare programme. Two types of cutbacks can be identified. First, there are the reductions in payments within programmes which have seen an overall increase. In this category are the changes in unemployment benefits within a total social security bill which has increased from £19,400 million in 1979–80 to £26,618 million in 1981–2. This increase has not been in the form of greater benefits for individual recipients. It would have been higher but for the fact that earnings-related benefits have been phased out, there is now no longer any statutory duty to raise unemployment benefit in line with price increases and the taxation of short-term benefits has been introduced. The effect is shown in Table 4.2; while more unemployment benefits are being paid, individual recipients are receiving less.

Second, there are the cutbacks in programmes which have been reduced as a whole. Some of the largest cutbacks have been borne by the housing programme which was cut back from an estimated out-turn of £4,672 million in 1980–1 to an estimated expenditure of £2,860 million in 1984–5. The

TABLE 4.2   *The changing value of unemployment benefits**

Year	Unemployment benefit	Unemployment benefit + earnings-related supplement
November 1978	20.28	35.23
November 1979	20.30	33.32
November 1980	19.45	31.40

*Equivalent value of April 1980 prices (£).

SOURCE: DHSS.

greatest savings are to be made by the reduction in subsidies to local authorities and the lack of capital expenditure in new local authority house-building. The net effect will be to increase council house rents and reduce the housing opportunities of those unable to afford owner-occupation.

Increases in education spending are to be slowed down. In cash terms spending on education increased by over 25 per cent between 1978–9 and 1981–2 but is planned to be less than 10 per cent between 1981–2 and 1984–5. These cutbacks and slow-downs are having real effects. The impact of restraint on education expenditure is for example noted in a report by Her Majesty's Inspectors (HMI):

... many LEAs (local education authorities) and schools are surviving financially by doing less; but they are often obliged to take the less if the form comes easily to hand rather than shaping it to match educational priorities. This means, in some cases, a general retrenchment in which most services, schools and pupils are affected to some degree ... Schools and pupils in deprived and disadvantaged areas are adversely affected by a combination of factors including old and deteriorating buildings, sharp falls in pupil numbers, reductions in specialist help for pupils with learning difficulties, cuts in ancillary staff such as nursing assistance and classroom helpers, and the absence of alternative sources of funding from, and support within, the community.

Schools are turning increasingly to parents and the local community for financial and other help. Funds are now frequently used to provide basic materials and equipment. This trend is leading to marked disparities of provision between schools serving affluent and poor areas.' (HMI, 1982, p. 13)

A similar sort of tale can be told for health where the general story is one of abandonment of new building projects, growing hospital waiting-lists and in certain inner city areas the complete closure of some medical facilities.

The general conclusion to be drawn is that the restraints and cutbacks on expenditure are being made in the social welfare programmes. Table 4.3 shows the general pattern of a decline in the proportion of public expenditure being spent on health, education and housing between 1976–7 and 1980–1 and further reductions for 1984–5 announced in the Conservative government's 1982 Budget. These reductions are not simply making the welfare services more efficient, cutting waste and dead wood; they are having real effects on real people. The most specific conclusion that can be drawn is that the greatest burdens are being faced by the most disadvantaged. The unskilled workers are more likely to be unemployed, to face increased council house rents, have poorer medical facilities, their children are likely to go to school where standards are falling and increased charges for health services are likely to constitute a larger proportion of income. Expenditure cutbacks are spinning a web of multiple deprivation as a generation of rising living standards is being halted and turned back on the road of fiscal purity towards falling living standards, deteriorating life chances and increased inequality.

These reductions have provoked responses. Five in particular can be identified.

Fight-backs. There have been organised responses to the more obvious effects. Parents and teachers have organised against the shut-down of schools and health workers and community organisers have picketed outside hospitals scheduled for closure. It has been much more difficult to fight against the steady, constant deterioration in public services. People may

TABLE 4.3 *Social welfare expenditure*

| | % of public expenditure | | |
| | Estimated out-turn | | Plan |
	1976–7	1980–1	1984–5
Health, education and housing	30.6	29.3	24.5

SOURCE: Treasury (1982) *The Government's Expenditure Plans 1982–83, to 1984–85*, Cmnd 8495 (London: HMSO).

take direct, collective action against the bus route being closed but only complain as individuals as older, slower public transport buses lumber along less frequently and charge more.

Opting out. The decline in the public welfare service has forced some of those who can afford it to opt out into the private sector. Private medicine and education for example have increased enormously in recent years and for those employed by some of the larger corporations, work-based medical schemes are important. The NHS still is left with the more expensive medical provision for mental illness, geriatric cases, etc. For those left out of the warming glow of corporate capitalism it has been a case of either using private resources to obtain better facilities or joining the growing queues.

Dissatisfaction. A pervasive response not incompatible with the first two has been a general rise in disatisfaction with the public welfare sectors. The early post-war dream of the welfare state has become the drab reality of declining services and harassed staff. Staff have become dispirited, morale is low and for most people their contact with the social welfare system has been an experience not of collective improvement but of despondency as they encounter dingy surroundings, tired and overworked staff. Throughout the past ten years the dream of the welfare state has faded. Many people have become dissatisfied and it has become much more difficult to organise resistance against cutbacks and easier for the government to reduce the commitment to and expenditure on the welfare services. There is still, however, a residuum of public commitment to the basics of the welfare state. The leaking of a Central Policy Review Staff document on reducing public expenditure in September 1982 which proposed amongst a number of alternatives the abolition of the NHS caused a public outcry sufficient for the Conservative Prime Minister to reaffirm in principle, if perhaps not in practice, the government's belief in the NHS. The incident revealed the political limits to public expenditure reductions. But the fact that the issue was even considered, even in a sort of fiscal worst-case scenario reveals how far we have travelled since the early 1960s.

The voice of the pump primers. The humanitarian arguments of the defenders of government welfare expenditure have received little sympathy from a nation which considers itself overtaxed. More purchase on informed opinion has been made by the arguments of the unions and sections of capital for the need for more government expenditure on capital spending programmes such as motorways, hospitals, schools, etc. The restraint on public expenditure has involved a disproportionate reduction in capital expenditure (see Table 4.4). Abandoning new or proposed capital projects is an easier way of achieving expenditure restraint than the renegotiation or reduction of existing commitments. Very few people complain of a school that was only an idea in the minds of the bureaucrats; there are, however, enough teachers in the

TABLE 4.4   *Capital expenditure*

	1976–7	1979–80	Plan 1982–3
Capital expenditure as a % of total public expenditure	16.7	14.0	10.1

SOURCE: Treasury (1982) *The Government's Expenditure Plans 1982–83 to 1984–85*, Cmnd 8494 (London: HMSO).

National Union of Teachers (NUT) to lobby against staff reductions in existing schools. The net result has been the deterioration of the nation's infrastructure as sewers, railways, roads, schools and hospitals age and are not replaced. The main unions concerned have long argued for more investment. One of the main arguments of the National Union of Railwaymen (NUR), for example, has been the need for investment in railways. Sections of capital, especially construction industry, also see merit and business in this scheme. Greater spending on capital programmes has attracted a fair measure of support across the range of interests from public sector unions through opinion-forming Keynesian economists to major industrial companies in the CBI. There are a number of arguments for a capital expenditure programme: it would create productive jobs and it would not suck in imports and hence cause a balance-of-payments problem, besides the infrastructure will have to be replaced some time. Spending on physical infrastructure is less ideologically loaded than spending on welfare programmes and thus has a greater measure of support. The demand for a programme of public capital expenditure is one that is gaining currency in influential circles.

Taking to the streets. In 1980 and 1981 a series of civil disturbances upset the normally quiet calm Britain gives off to its many tourists. The image of shabby gentility, of a poor but affable society was swept aside by images of youths fighting with police. Whatever the real reasons were, and we will discuss them later, it was commonly believed that high unemployment and lack of opportunities were important ingredients. The government responded by putting more money into the inner cities through the Urban Aid Programme and partnership schemes and increasing the spending of the Manpower Services Commission on youth unemployment schemes. Disorder in the streets was not an explicit argument against the government's economic policies. But the deeper causes showed the limits and the consequences of reducing government spending on certain services at a time of deepening recession in the private sector. The maintenance of social harmony is an important state function. In times of recession it involves some expenditure and it places limits on the drive to reduce spending on welfare programmes.

(2) *Central–local relations in hard times*

The perceived need for central government to control local government expenditure has arisen because of the government's aim to control public spending. A significant proportion of total spending is made by local authorities. In 1980–1 out of a total of £93,475 million spent by the government, local authorities spent £25,109 million, approximately 27 per cent. Throughout the 1970s local authority spending constituted approximately one-quarter of all public spending. Local authority spending has increased because of the demands for service provision made by central government on local authorities, the increased demand by users for local authority services, the improvement of services and increases in the cost of providing services. The costs are highest in the urban areas; the most expensive local government is urban local government.

Many of the public services which have been guaranteed and expanded in post-war Britain have been provided by the local authorities. Table 4.5 shows how local authorities are the main provider of education, environmental services (planning, pro-

TABLE 4.5   *Local authorities' spending by programme, 1980–1*

	£m	as % of all government spending
Education, arts and libraries	9495	83.4
Environmental services	2568	76.0
Law, order and protective services	2380	74.8
Housing	2568	54.9
Transport	1990	57.0
Health and personal social services	1697	14.9
Social security	370	1.5
Agriculture, fisheries, food and forestry	169	12.2
Industry, energy, trade and employment	131	3.1

SOURCE: *Economic Trends.*

vision of parks, swimming pools, etc.), law and order and housing. For all these programmes local authority spending constitutes more than half of all government spending. Over 80 per cent of local spending is current spending, most of it taken up in salaries. Over half the total education bill for example is spent on wages. The capital spending, financed by borrowing, is concentrated in the housing sector on the construction of council housing.

The ability of central government to control local spending has arisen because local authorities have become dependent upon central government for income. Local authorities get their money from local property taxes (rates), government grants and borrowing from the money market. Rates are levied on occupiers of non-agricultural land and building. But like all tax sources of revenue there are political limits to the amount which can be raised through rates. Massive rate increases in 1974–6 for example prompted a political and public outcry leading to the setting up of the Layfield Commission in 1974.

Borrowing by local authorities has been high. In 1980–1 for example local authority borrowing amounted to £1,237 million, 9.3 per cent of the PSBR. This borrowing has to be paid for and interest charges in 1980–1 amounted to £4,367 million, comprising 17.3 per cent of total local authority spending; debt charges are the single biggest expenditure after education. Local authorities cannot borrow indefinitely. On the one hand there are the crippling interest payments and on the other there are central government controls on local authority borrowing.

With political limits to rate increases and statutory limits on borrowing the local authorities have been dependent on central government grants to finance growing expenditure. These grants as a proportion of local authority receipts have grown from a third in the 1950s to almost half by the late 1970s. The disparity between the getting and spending of money for local authorities has placed them in a position dependent on the central government.

With growing fiscal difficulties and the growing size of local government spending programmes, successive central governments have felt it necessary to control local government expenditure. The methods have become more Draconian as the perceived fiscal crisis has increased. Prior to the mid 1970s the methods took the form of organisational reform. In the early 1960s, for example, government asked local authorities to develop capital expenditure programmes up to five years ahead. In 1967 following the devaluation crisis a new government grant – the Rate Support Grant (RSG) – was given to local authorities on a supposedly more rational basis to take into account the variations in need and resources between local authorities. In practice the RSG was susceptible to manipulation, because the formulae used to distribute it could be changed to favour certain types of local authorities. During the period of a Labour government (1974–8) the RSG was adjusted to aid the urban, Labour-dominated areas. The Conservative government of 1979 readjusted the formula to give more to Shire counties. The largest measure was the reorganisation of local government passed in 1972 and implemented in 1974. The aim was to create larger, more efficient, more cost-effective units of government. Associated with local government reform were attempts at introducing corporate management in order to aid efficiency and reduce costs. Since local government was big business it should act, according to the management reformers, like big business (Bennington, 1976).

The mid 1970s marked a second stage in central–local relations as central government sought to achieve restraint in public spending through greater control of local government expenditure. From 1975 cash limits were introduced and local authorities were no longer given supplements to the RSG. The rest of the 1970s is a story of cuts, as cash limits were set with assumptions of relatively low inflation.

Throughout the later 1970s local authorities were caught in the pincers of rising expenditure due to increase in the cost of service provision and high inflation on the one hand, and on the other, loss of government grant. They all responded by increasing fees and charges for local government services (e.g. swimming pool entrance fees, etc.) while some increased rates. With the worsening fiscal crisis and a return of a Conservative government in 1979 a new era in the relationship between central and local government was inaugurated. The Tories very quickly set themselves the task of putting a fiscal cap to local government spending. Under the financial provisions of the 1980 Local Government, Planning and Land Act both capital and current spending were placed under greater central control. Capital spending was to be subject to a ceiling set each year while under revenue spending a new block grant replaced the RSG. Under the block grant system a spending limit was placed and if local authorities went above this limit central government grants would tail off. In 1981 a local government bill was launched whose aim was to place limits on local authorities' ability to finance spending over and above the limits placed by central government. The first version contained proposals for a referendum to be held before supplementary rates could be levied. In a second version, introduced after much parliamentary debate and opposition from local authority representatives, especially the Association of Metropolitan Authorities, the idea of a referendum was dropped and a banning of supplementary rates instituted instead. Under the 1981 Local Authority Finance Act the Secretary of the State can penalise the authorities deemed to have overspent. In theory the legislation was meant to control local government spending. In practice it was used to penalise the higher spending Labour-controlled, urban authorities whose expenditure patterns with their high social welfare components were out of tune with the new Right of the Conservative party. In reality, the central–local dispute was overlain by political and ideological divisions. Rather than a simple fiscal exercise it was an exercise in political control and an example of ideological dispute.

In 1982 central government had gained the necessary powers to restrain local government spending. The costs were high. There were serious tensions between central and local authorities especially between the Labour-dominated Association of Metropolitan Authorities and the government. But even some Tory back-benchers and councillors and the more Right-wing Association of County Councils and the Association of District Councils were wary of the new legislation with its strong centralised powers. Although it was debatable whether the legislation marked the death-knell of local government democracy it certainly signalled greater limits on local government autonomy.

(3) *Public sector employees and the fiscal crisis*

The growth of government in post-war Britain has involved
more than a rising level of public spending and a groaning pile
of official documents. One of its most tangible effects has been
the growth in the number of people employed by the state.
Today just over one in every four persons employed works for
the government. The government is not just the biggest
spender, it is now the biggest employer. The government wage
bill now constitutes a significant proportion of total government expenditure. Figure 4.5, which shows the figures for
1981–2, reveals that just over a quarter of general government
expenditure (almost £3500 million) went on wages and
salaries.

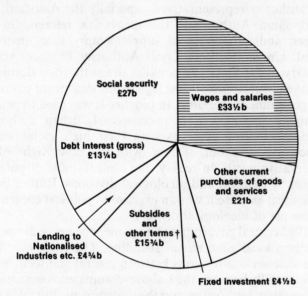

FIGURE 4.5   *Central and local government expenditure, 1981–2**

* Total cash expenditure: £120 billion.
† Other items include industrial and regional assistance, current grants
abroad, student awards, grants to universities and lending for house
purchase.

SOURCE: Treasury (1982) *The Government's Expenditure Plans 1982–83 to
1984–85*, Cmnd 8494 (London: HMSO).

The growth of public sector employment has involved the growth of public sector unions. The growth of the labour force in union membership (from 38.6 per cent in 1945 to 52.1 per cent in 1970) has mainly been a result of the high levels of unionisation in public sector employment. Unionisation is easier and has often been encouraged in government employment. Apart from the typically high levels of unionisation in the old public service sectors of railways, steelworks and mines, the 1960s and 1970s witnessed the very fast growth of the new public sector unions covering teachers, local government officers and health service workers. The NHS is now the largest single employer in western Europe. Like all unions, public service unions, both new and old, are established and operate to protect their members' jobs and living standards.

Throughout the 1960s and 1970s there has been a series of clashes between these unions and the government. Prior to the mid 1970s the issues revolved around incomes policies and pay restraint. A major source of industrial unrest and strike action of the past twenty years has been the attempt by government to impose wage limits on public sector unions. The flurry of strike action in the late 1960s and early 1970s was successful in ensuring increased wages as inflation continued to rise. The success of the union proved an invaluable recruiting sergeant as more and more workers sought protection from the ravages of inflation in the unions.

Since the mid 1970s there has been renewed tension between the government and the public sector unions. The intellectual climate has been transformed by the new monetarism and the explicit anti-public sector stance of major opinion-makers. The work of two economists, Bacon and Eltis (1976, 1978) has proved to be very influential. In the first edition of their work they argued that the economy could be divided into two sectors: the marketed and non-marketed sectors. The marketed sector comprises all those goods and services for sale (cars, washing-machines, etc.) while the non-marketed sector provides goods and services (such as schools, police, etc.) which are either not sold or are sold well below the real cost of provision. The former was associated by Bacon and Eltis with the private sector and the latter with the public sector. The two economists then went on to argue that the growth of the non-marketed sector reduced the share of, and increased claims on, the marketed output of the economy. In other words, much of the growth of the public sector was a growth of unproductive services and workers, diverting resources away from the real source of wealth, the private sector. Bacon and Eltis in effect drew a causal connection between Britain's continuing poor economic performance and the growth of the public sector. A solution to Britain's economic problems' they argued, thus lay in reducing the size and cost of the public sector. This general argument was shared by many senior politicians and in a speech in September 1975 Margaret Thatcher emphasised the Conservative's position:

> The private sector creates the goods and services we need both to export, to pay for our imports and the revenue to finance public services. So one must not overload it. Every man switched away from industry and into government will reduce the productive sector and increase the burden on it at the same time.

Of course Bacon and Eltis in reaching their conclusions ignored the benefits to the private sector of the public sector. The latter socialised much of the costs of material production and social reproduction. In the second edition of their work they slightly revised their position. Initially they had assumed full employment. Workers 'released' from government could thus be absorbed by the private sector. But in conditions of high unemployment, as they noted in 1978, workers released might not be absorbed. The choice thus lay between government employment and unemployment.

There is now a climate of opinion which sees a definite need to reduce the growth of the public sector. Nowhere is this more strongly expressed than in the Conservative party which sees it as a duty to curb the power of the public sector unions. While in opposition in the 1970s the Conservatives were drawing up plans which they were then to implement in office. In 1978 a secret report drawn up by Nicholas Ridley indicated the new tough line. Nationalised industries were to achieve higher rates of return and wages were to be based on productivity. The report realised however that unions wielded considerable power and went on to argue that the next Conservative government should choose carefully the public sector unions to take on over a wage claim. Public sector unions were thus classified for this purpose by the degree of 'vulnerability of the nation to strike action'. A three-fold classification was established:

(1) *Most vulnerable*. The unions in this category included sewerage workers, water workers, electricity, gas and health service workers. The government was to avoid a head-on collision.
(2) *Intermediate*. Railway workers, dock workers and miners.
(3) *Least vulnerable*. This included workers in the public transport, education, telephones, air transport and steel industries.

The Ridley report may have been used as a basis for action in the first years of the Conservative government that was elected in 1979. The report identified steel workers as not a great threat. In early 1980 the steel workers asked for a 19.7 per cent wage rise but the British Steel Corporation (BSC) offered only 14.4 per cent. There then followed a four-month strike in which the government refused to intervene. After an independent enquiry and appointment of another BSC Chairman, a new plan for steel was introduced in late 1980 which called for the immediate loss of 20,000 jobs and a gradual reduction of the labour force from 150,000 to 100,000.

From the mid 1970s onwards the tension between government and the public sector unions also sharpened with the use of cash limits. Previously each spending department put in an annual estimate of its expenditure using existing pay and price levels. Departments would then submit supplementary estimates to cover subsequent pay and price increases. This was an open-ended form of public expending. Pay increases if allowed were paid automatically and they were only subject to the succession of pay freezes and incomes policies tried and eventually found wanting by successive governments. With the introduction of cash limits in 1976 the government placed a cap in advance on the amount to be spent by the various departments. Although incomes policies have come and gone, cash limits seem to be here to stay. Pay policies are now controlled through cash limits because, since these limits specify a given level of pay increase in the next fiscal year, if the pay claim is greater than the specified amount in the cash limits the government argues that the 'extra' can only be paid if non-pay items are reduced or there is a reduction in manpower. Since the mid 1970s then public sector unions have attempted to fight against both job losses and wage reductions pursued by governments who believe that the public sector is a drain on resources. The government in turn has sought to restrain spending by enforcing cash limits. In 1981–2 cash limits made provision for only 6 per cent pay increases and the cash limits for 1982–3 were based on only 4 per cent pay increases. The representatives of the government around pay bargaining tables have told the unions that awards over and above the assumed rates can only be made if there are reductions in staff or non-pay expenditure. The aim of the unions in turn has been to increase the wages while holding staffing constant. There have been some union successes; in 1980–1 the National and Local Government Officers' Association (NALGO) achieved a $7\frac{1}{2}$ per cent pay increase compared to the 6 per cent offered and in February 1981 the threat of a miners' strike forced the Conservative government to increase the level of funding to the National Coal Board to avoid pit closures. But there have also been some union failures: witness the case of British Steel. The success of a particular union depends upon their industrial muscle, ther organisational strength, the amount of money in the union coffers and the exchequer and the disposition of both government and public. The outcome of a particular conflict cannot be predicted in advance. There are too many contingencies. What remains an absolute, however, is the fact that the 1980s will continue to be a period of unrest. At the time of writing (Summer 1982) there has been a strike in the main railway union, the NUR, followed by the train drivers' dispute, British Airways announced a cut of 7,000 jobs, and most public service unions are pledging to fight against compulsory redundancies suggested by the next round of cash limits. The most dramatic conflict has occurred between the government and the health service unions. A union day of action called in support of the health services union in September 1982 saw over two and a half million workers out in sympathy and a demonstration in London attracted 120,000 supporters.

Most official searches for the solution of the fiscal crisis of the state take the route of cuts in public spending, public jobs and public pay. While this may lessen public expenditure it increases social tension. The solution of the fiscal crisis of the state is more than just an accountant's dilemma, involving as it does social and political conflict.

Reproducing the social order

Societies reproduce themselves. Each generation is socialised individually through family, friends, acquaintances, and collectively through shared experiences, the consumption of mass media and passages through the education system. The state plays an enormous role in all this; the provision of education and health services, the control of mass media and the ultimate sanction in the power of the police and the rule of law gives the state a pivotal position in the reproduction of the social order. Indeed in many cases the state is the social order. The regular elections reproduce the political order and much of the state's actions are aimed at maintaining the economic order. The state's role becomes particularly acute when the social order is undergoing severe strain. The ending of the boom with the loss of full employment, decline in expectations, falling living standards and reductions in public expenditure have lead to the vitiation of political consensus and the production of new stresses. We can examine these with respect to education, law and order and in the relationship between the state and the mass media.

Education

The state is in charge of education. Education is controlled partly by central government, which administers secondary and primary curricula through directives from the Department of Education and funds the universities through the University Grants Committee, and partly by the local authorities which provide the buildings, cash and teachers for primary, secondary and some tertiary education through the local education authority. In any society schools socialise the next and succeeding generations into the values, knowledge and mores of that society. There is however no simple process of indoctrination in contemporary Britain. To believe that is to believe too much in the ability of the state to achieve its ends. The education system is not simply a transmission belt taking status quo apologetics from the top to the middle and bottom of the social hierarchy, it is a source of tension in its own right.

In the first place, teachers have become a unionised body of workers who have sought to fight against reductions in their wages as part of the general strategy of reducing public expenditure and public sector wages in particular. Moreover, teachers vary in their ideology and in their collective experiences. The younger teachers of the late 1960s, 1970s and early 1980s have proved to be a radicalising experience for some pupils. In the second place, the education system itself is failing to produce the numbers of qualified people. The education system in Britain seems to have been designed to produce a relatively small number of well-educated people to manage industry, staff the senior levels of the civil service and in general run the country. The passage from primary school to secondary school to university is followed by less than 10 per cent of the population. For the rest education begins at primary and ends at secondary. The system seems designed to fail a significant minority of its participants. Approximately 50 per cent of children left school in 1980 without at least one 'O' level. Sixty-seven per cent leave secondary school at the minimum leaving age and over 50 per cent have become almost permanent truants in their last year. The system worked relatively well in its own terms (although not in terms of realising individual potential) in the 1950s and 1960s as the mass of school-leavers were picked up despite their low attainment by a booming economy and given a ride on the escalator of rising real incomes. Particularly significant was the burgeoning middle class for whom a booming economy allowed a direct relationship between educational attainment and job advancement. With the decline of the economy has come the slump, which as we saw in Chapter 3 has been particularly bad for the school-leavers especially for those with few recognisable qualifications. The education system is now under pressure from a number of sides. In the latter years of the secondary schools there is the problem of how to handle the early leavers who have no hope, few job prospects and little interest. Their resentment is not collectively articulated but expressed at the individual level and in a few cases is the driving power behind vandalism and random violence. There is also the pressure from the parents who want their children to gain qualifications, the necessary prerequisite for career prospects. The more affluent parents are more articulate, shout loudest and lobby most effectively. The very rich and/or very ambitious have opted out of the state system altogether and send their children to private schools where educational attainment is, it is hoped, part of the fees. Private schools have an importance way beyond their numbers. The exact definition of the ruling élite or governing body in contemporary Britain may vary but what is without question is that the vast majority of its members have been socialised in the world of private education which is outside the experience of the rest of the population.

The demand for more educational spending expressed by parents and teachers is a recognition that educational attainment is as much a function of public expenditure as a private achievement. By influencing the level of educational spending the state influences levels of educational attainment. This is particularly noticeable at the local level where a whole series of studies have demonstrated the relationship between local authority spending and educational attainment (see Kirby, 1982). The state also has a direct influence through the curriculum. Two aspects of the curriculum debate can be identified. First, there is the campaign of the political Right on the type of subjects taught. Tory MPs, councillors and teachers can always be relied upon to criticise sociology, critical studies of government and the lack of 'proper' moral teaching in schools; criticism of sociology is *de rigueur* for Conservatives who want to get on in public life. But concerned teachers have brought contemporary concerns into the classroom through social history, current affairs, economics and human geography. Second, there has been the much larger discussion over the exact jobs schools should be doing. The 'Great Debate' started in 1976 concerned itself with the relationship between education and industry. Education, so it was argued, should be more responsive to the needs of industry, and the image of a hide-bound, civil service-dominated education mentality was touted around by critics and would-be reformers. The precise form of the link between schools and work has not been made but the debate has highlighted some of the more obvious failings of the British education system; an education system which seems geared to generating failure, overspecialisation and a lack of technical training. In the depths of the current recession however it is difficult to argue that schools are not producing the right set of employees although the inability of the schools to produce people cognisant of modern technology is now well recognised. Rather, the economy seems not to be producing the right number of jobs.

The state has a number of jobs to perform and interests to meet in education. On the one hand there are demands for more education spending by parents, teachers and the educational establishment. These interests are expressed particularly at the local level. And on the other hand industrial capital would like less welfare expenditure and round pegs for their round holes. These interests are strongly articulated at the central government level. The reproduction of a social order through the education system is not a simple manner of indoctrination as the conflict of interests and the emerging tensions are felt here as elsewhere.

Law

The social order is bound by the law which gives legal consent to some actions and withholds it from others. In the unwritten British constitution, statute law, laid down by parliamentary legislation, is the ultimate authority and overrides custom and common law (laid down by precedent and judicial interpretation). In theory, therefore, parliament has the final say in the constitutional set-up. Thus, if the theory is correct the officers of the law simply implement parliamentary and, more acurately, government wishes. To a certain extent the theory is true. The government appoints members of the judiciary through the Lord Chancellor who is a member of the Cabinet, pays them their wages and employs them in a variety of extra-judicial roles in committees and royal commissions. In return judges uphold the rule of law. And the law itself takes the interests of state as paramount. I say the interests of state rather than government since this implies a more long-standing constant set of concerns with authority relations rather than the sometimes ephemeral business of transient governments. The judiciary is obsessed with 'the necessity to protect and preserve the structures of constitutional authority without undue concern for the rights of those who wish to challenge that authority' (Griffith, 1981, p. 219).

The laws and their implementation reinforce and codify social and political power in society, especially in common law where precedent and judicial interpretation provide the context. The implementation of the law reflects the prevailing ideology which is the discourse of entrenched social and economic power. The law criminalises threats to the existing order. Crime and the rule of law are not arbitrary, they have a political meaning and social consequences. Thus it comes as no surprise that the implementation of the law in Britain is concerned with 'the maintenance of order, the protection of private property, the promotion of certain general economic aims, the containment of the trade union movement and the continuance of governments which conduct their business largely in private and on the advice of other members of . . . the governing group' (Griffith, 1981, p. 240).

But the judiciary is not merely the neutral transmitter of government wishes. Statute law allows a great deal of compass in interpretation while common law is a process of continual interpretation. In a well-argued thesis Griffith has shown how in their implementation role the judiciary was and is an independent source of power and their interpretation has always protected big property interests and big capital; the judges have supported the status quo.

The independent role of the judiciary, which invalidates constitutional theory as taught, has been silhouetted more clearly by recent events. Three main trends can be identified. First, there has been a challenge to the existing order throughout the 1960s and 1970s in the form of strikes, squatting, demonstrations and other challenges to governmental power. Griffith demonstrates 'that in every major social issue which has come before the courts during the last thirty years – concerning industrial relations, political protest, race relations, governmental secrecy, police powers, moral behaviour – the judges have supported the conventional, established and settled interests' (p. 239–40). Those seeking a lead in social reform will look in vain at the British judiciary.

Second, the existing order itself has been subject to change. The post-war years have seen different signals coming from the state as governments replaced governments and different policies prevailed. For example, in 1975, Tameside, a Labour-controlled council, approved plans for comprehensive schools. In May 1976 the Conservatives won control of the council and proposed not to carry out the plans. The Education Secretary of the Labour government took the council to court and the divisional court ordered the council to comply with the minister's rulings. The Court of Appeal overturned the decision and the Law Lords upheld the Court of Appeal's ruling. In 1981, a Labour-controlled Greater London Council (GLC), explicitly campaigning on the very issue, reduced the fares of London Transport. Bromley Borough Council objected, took the matter to court and the Court of Appeal and the Law Lords both agreed that the GLC could not increase fares. The two cases are interesting in that they show how the judges overrule ministerial intervention on the one case and the wishes of a democratically elected authority on the other. Their reasoning, stripped of the legalistic verbiage has been shown to be unsound, unreasoned and simply the justification of existing practice. In the case of the GLC, for example, the Law Lords while being acutely aware of the costs to the ratepayers were completely ignorant of the social costs in transport considerations. The judiciary would seem to be expressing, through interpretation of statute law, an independent source of power to block radical and democratic changes to the status quo. The judiciary is the long-stop in the fielding side of the establishment.

Third, enacted legislation has been political by its very nature. Industrial relations legislation for example has placed the judiciary in an explicitly political position since the interpretation of the law can effect the balance of advantage to either capital or labour. Through its manning of the ill-fated

National Industrial Relations Court and in its interpretation of industrial relations legislation the judiciary has favoured capital against labour and the state against its workforce.

And order

Governments and parts of the state apparatus are challenged with upholding law and order. In post-war Britain the story of law and order is an interesting one, reflecting as it does the tensions opening up in a society with a declining economic base. The broad outlines of the story are well known: the post-war years have seen an increase in the official crime statistics, the promotion of law and order to a key position in social commentary and political ideology, the rise of police power and influence and more recently a consequent backlash. Let us examine these in some detail.

The official statistics suggest an upward trend in reported crimes. Figure 4.6 for example shows the steady post-war rise in serious offences (these are offences involving violence against the person, sexual offences, burglary, theft and handling stolen goods, fraud and forgery, criminal damage, blackmail and libel) Violent crime is increasing as is the use of

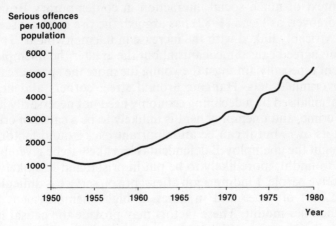

FIGURE 4.6 *Serious crime statistics, England and Wales*

SOURCE: *Criminal Statistics.*

firearms. Serious offences recorded by the police in which firearms were reported increased from 1,734 in England and Wales in 1971 to 6,547 in 1981. The main increase in criminal activity has come from the younger age groups: in 1980 there were almost eighty serious offences per 1,000 in the age group 14–16; only ten per 1,000 in the over-21 age group. The statistics seem plain, the explanations are more difficult. The question why remains a difficult one to answer. We have to be wary of the statistical problems involved. The increase in crimes reported may be a function of a more efficient police service. The inexorable rise in crime may be more an indication of police efficiency than of societal breakdown. Moreover, the definitions and prosecution of crimes have varied over time. The police and the courts are now more sensitised to juvenile crime and violent offences and their increase may be to some extent a result of greater police vigilance. Despite these caveats it is now a part of accepted folklore that there has been a rise in crime. Part of this increase may be caused by that complex set of attitudes which inform individual social action. The decline in informal social control as old neighbourhoods are destroyed and lose their cohesion and family units no longer remain stable in association with the steady drip-feed of sanctioned and sanitised violence on television has no doubt changed the context of much social interaction in contemporary Britain. Moreover, as Dean (1982) has argued, the rise of crime seems inextricably linked with the increase in unemployment. There is no agreed causal mechanism, but the greater the unemployment especially amongst the young the more the space created for criminal acts. Hanging around street corners and being marginalised by a declining economy need not necessarily lead to crime, and unemployment is unlikely to be a cause of crime on its own, but it can be an important background factor. If caught the unemployed defendent is less likely to be given bail, or to find it, more likely to be put in prison and less likely to receive parole. Finding a job after a prison service is difficult at the best of times and in times of high unemployment the difficulties mount. These factors may provide the causal link between the accepted statistical relationship between recidivism and unemployment.

In terms of the response to rise in crime we have to

distinguish the exact sequence of events. The commonsense view is that the post-war story is one of rising crime leading to public disquiet and a widening and deepening of police powers. In an important book, Hall *et al.* (1978) question this cosy assumption. In their attempt to explain the insertion of law and order to the front page of an agenda of public issue topics, Hall *et al.* argue that in the 1950s the post-war construction of consensus based on social welfare provision and rising real incomes was built upon an unstable moral basis. In this rapidly changing world there was a loss of moral markers, rising social unease at the pace and scale of change most keenly felt and articulated by what they term the 'lumpen bourgeoise'. For this group the increase in working-class living standards, the new-found confidence of the 'lower orders' and the loss of deference were a source of disquiet. This unease fastened onto specific issues; the problems of youth and the Teddy boy cult. And in the 1950s there was a series of moral panics concerning the decline of the family and parental control and the growth of hooliganism essentially directed at working-class youths. Throughout the 1960s, Hall *et al.* argue, we can see the beginnings of the decline of the economic boom and the sharpening of industrial and class conflict. The mid 1960s mark a turning-point in which the unease of the lower middle classes and the threats to the existing moral order become manifest and there is a rising tide of opinion against 'permissiveness', all fuelled and amplified by the moral entrepreneurs through the media. Law and order becomes part of this discourse as spokesmen argue for the need to stand firm. By the early 1970s this language has captured the experience of rising industrial militancy, squats, student unrest and terrorism in one inter-linked and causally related threat to the established order,

the war in Bangladesh, Cyprus, the Middle East, Black September, Black Power, the Angry Brigade, the Kennedy murders, Northern Ireland, bombs in Whitehall and the Old Bailey, the Welsh Language Society, the massacre in the Sudan, the muggings in the tube, gas strikes, hospital strikes, go-slows, sit-in's, the Icelandic cod war were all standing or seeking to stand on different parts of the same slippery slope. (quoted in Griffith, 1974)

The demand for law and order and stronger police powers became not just a reaction to a perceived crime wave but a refractor for social tensions and class conflict, a prism for individual fears about crime, real and imagined. By the mid 1960s and early 1970s, Hall *et al.* argue, the law and order debate rather than being a function of rising crime sensitised the public to the issue. In that sense it was partly a cause.

Throughout the 1970s we see the insertion of the law and order debate to an important position in public debate. Successive governments pledged themselves to a war on crime, with the Conservative party taking the lead backed by pressure from its supporters and back-benchers. The experience of strikes, squats and industrial militancy was captured as just one more element of this disorder to be halted only by stronger police powers and larger sentences for offenders. As the economic crisis deepens, the law and order debate widens to include the organised power of labour and political 'extremism' of the Left. The campaign has its Folk Devil:

the 'mugger' was such a Folk Devil; his form and shape accurately reflected the content of the fears and anxieties of those who first imagined, and then actually discovered him: young, black, bred in or arising from the 'breakdown of social order' in the city; threatening the traditional peace of the streets, the security of movement of the ordinary respectable citizen; motivated by naked gain, a reward he would come by, if possible, without a days honest toil; his crime, the outcome of a thousand occasions when adults and parents had failed to correct, civilise and tutor his wilder impulses; impelled by an even more frightening need for 'gratuitous violence', an inevitable result of the weakening of moral fibre in family and society, and the general collapse of respect for discipline and authority. In short, the very token of 'permissiveness' embodying in his every action and person, feelings and values that were the opposite of those decencies and restraints which make England what she is. (Hall *et al.*, 1978, pp. 161–2)

Hall *et al.* argue that the post-war story in Britain is a story of a move from consensus to coercion, one of a crisis in authority marked by a shift in a series of moral panics to a law and order society. To an extent their claim is justified if we consider the development of policing in post-war Britain.

The post-war years have seen the growth, specialisation and reorganisation of the police. In 1961 there were 87,900 police excluding auxillaries and by 1980 this figure had increased to 137,5000. Until 1964 there were 126 local police forces in England and Wales and forty-two in Scotland but after local government reorganisation there were only forty-two in England and Wales and eight in Scotland. The growth in size and power of the police forces has not been counterbalanced by greater accountability. Local councils through their police committees pay for the police force but have no control. In London the local boroughs have no control, the Metropolitan police come under Home Office jurisdiction. The police force has also become more car-bound and more specialised. The 'bobby on the beat', the embodiment of policing in a consensual society, has been replaced by the motor-cop firmly ensconced behind a driving wheel and desensitised from the nuances of the local community. An important development has been the growth of special groups within the police. The Special Branch, responsible for monitoring 'subversive' activities, has grown from 200-strong in the early 1960s to nearly 1,500 by 1980. The 1970s have also seen the growth of the Special Patrol Groups (SPG) trained in riot control, picket-breaking and 'heavy arm' tactics. They have been used in London's inner city areas for saturation policing. In November 1978 over 100 SPG officers were involved in stop and search operations, road blocks and mass arrests in Lambeth. In total 430 people were arrested for obstruction, alleged theft, suspicious activity and assaults on police officers. Forty per cent of those arrested were young blacks. In SWAMP 81 the SPG were involved in policing in force in the Brixton area; a preface to the riots. There has also been the growth of Police Support Units initially formed in 1973 as a unit of civil defence but transformed throughout the 1970s to deal with crowd control, riots and threats to public order. In one sense the growth of the Special Units signals a definite move from consensus to coercion. The organic links between Britain's police force and its population have not been completely broken however. In quieter rural areas for example consensus lingers on and police fill their traditional role. In the big cities in contrast the link has been broken by increasing size and specialisation of the police, the growth of paramilitary units and the tendency of police and image-makers to see all dissent including demonstrations, strikes, etc. as threats to the existing order.

The language of the law and order society has afforded a special role to the police. First, more has been spent on law and order serivices. Table 4.6, for example, contrasts public spending on law and order with that on education. Notice how spending on education has declined while that on law and order services has increased and much of this increase has come from the greater salary levels now paid to the police force. Greater spending on law and order was one of the main items in the Conservative manifesto of 1979. Given a small and shrinking public purse this increase has been purchased at the expense of other items of social policy. Second, criticism of the police centring on the lack of accountability, complaints of police brutality or charges of corruption have been dismissed. Not simply marked as untrue but also dangerous, as to criticise the police is to undermine their position. In the language of the law and order society, to criticise the police or to do more than simply parrot the phrases of 'best police force in the world', etc. is to take the side of the criminals, the mugger, the striker: to eat into the very moral fabric of society. This attitude, exemplified

TABLE 4.6   *Public spending on law and order and education*

	1970	1975–6	1978–9	1979–80	1981–2	1982
(A) *Total public expenditure (constant prices)* (1979–80 = 100)						
Law and order services		96	96	100	107	
Education		103	100	100	93	
(B) *Annual salary levels (£)*						
Police constable	1470					8883
Head teacher	2101					8769

SOURCE: Treasury (1982) *The Government's Expenditure Plans 1982–83 to 1984–85*, Cmnd 8494 (London: HMSO).

by every government spokesman who has ever made any public statement on the police has buttressed the position of the police who like any organisation immunised from criticism have grown in stature and influence. There has been a convergence of opinion between the police's own perspective of a healthy society being based on discipline and acceptance of authority and the language and ideology of the law and order society. As Thompson (1980) has noted:

> there is nothing new about Sir Robert Mark's or Sir David McNee's illiberal and impatient notions. What is new is the very powerful public relations operation which disseminates these notions as an authorised, consensual view – an operation carried on out of our own taxes; which presses its spokesman forward on every occasion upon the media; which lobbies enquiries and Royal Commissions, constantly pressing for larger powers; which bullies weak Home Secretaries (and boos them when they cross their wishes); which reproves magistrates for lenient sentencing; which announces unashamedly that the police are in the regular practice of breaking judges' rules when interrogating suspects; which slanders unnamed lawyers and lampoons libertarian organisations; which tells judges how they are to interpret the law; and which justifies the invasion of the citizens' privacy and the accumulation of prejudicial and inaccurate records.
> This is new. This is formidable. (p. 200–1)

The whole drift of the organised public attitude to the police has been to strengthen the hand of policemen like James Anderton, Chief Constable of Greater Manchester, who could condense complex debates into slogans and run off police interests with those of national security and the upholding of democracy. In a BBC programme (*Question Time*, broadcast on 16 October 1980) he said

> I think that from the police point of view . . . my task in the future, in the 10 to 15 years from now . . . that basic crimes such as theft, burglary, even violent crime will not be the

predominant police feature. What will be the matter of greatest concern to me will be the covert and ultimately overt attempts to overthrow democracy, to subvert the authority of the state, and to in fact involve themselves in acts of sedition designed to destroy a parliamentary system and the democratic government of this country.

The alternative, voiced by John Alderson, formerly Chief Constable of Devon and Cornwall, asking for more community policing, a greater reliance on consensus rather than coercion, was often heard but rarely listened to; that is until the summer riots of 1981.

The 1981 urban riots in Britain may mark a turning-point. The events in that year were prefaced by a riot in St Paul's, Bristol in 1980 when there were clashes between blacks and whites but mainly between young people and the police. In the next year there was a major riot in Brixton in which the main dimensions of the conflict were between young blacks and the police. Before this revolt Brixton had been heavily policed by the SPG in SWAMP 81. Later that summer riots occurred in Moss-side in Manchester, Toxteth in Liverpool and elsewhere. By the weekend of 10–12 July riots were taking place in a score of towns and cities throughout Britain. The official response was two-fold. First, there was the gut response of the law and order brigade. The Home Secretary, William Whitelaw, told Conservative back-benchers on 13 July that the police would be equipped with riot-control gas, rubber bullets and water cannons. He told the police to take the offensive. Second, a public enquiry was ordered under Lord Scarman who was appointed on 14 April 1981 to enquire into the Brixton disorder. Later riots were also covered. The Scarman report (1981) was interesting in two respects. On the one hand it pointed to the socio-economic context of the riots. Poor housing, poor education and poor unemployment prospects provided the tinder for the flames of disorder. Scarman noted that the life chances of many young people in inner city areas were limited and the riots were less of a race riot than 'a burst of anger'. On the other hand Scarman also directly and indirectly criticised the police. He pointed to the existence of racialism in the police force and called amongst other things for:

- more police recruitment of ethnic minorities
- better training and larger periods of probation for police officers
- more consultation between police forces and the community through statutory liaison committees.

The Scarman report was partial in its terms of reference. It excluded for example any consideration of British immigration policy. However, it was more than a mere whitewash. It pointed to the limits of a social policy which led to massive youth unemployment and declining public services, and the social costs of a shift from consensus to coercion policing in inner city areas. The proposals have yet to be implemented. Perhaps they never will. But the riots and the reports and the subsequent debate have shifted the parameters of the discussion. The trend towards an aggressively monetarist policy with heavy policing was not entirely halted but a glimpse had been given of the full social and political costs.

In an important book, Thompson (1980) has written a number of essays which point to the increasingly authoritarian strand in contemporary British political life. He points to the growth and influence of the secret service establishment and the law and order brigade with their implicit belief that a healthy society is one based on consensus, acceptance of authority and free from conflict. From this perspective tension does not arise naturally but is imported by extremists, bully-boys, militants and antisocial elements. The linking of amorphous popular and not so popular movements provides the authoritarian case for more control, less accountability and less freedom of information. The slide into authoritarianism is not led by armed thugs, modern-day Brownshirts. History rarely repeats itself:

> the brokers of repression will have been the television controllers who rushed forward to offer Dimbleby lectures and chat show places to the police; the MPs who could not, once in the matter of the jury, divide the house; the editors who served up every official hand-out in return for paltry inside leaks; the judges who, when asked for justice, gave us back a hole; and all the law-and-order brigade, warming

their hands before the burning constitution. (Thompson, 1980, p. 251)

It is a bleak image. Whether it will turn into an ugly reality only time will tell but there are a number of important counter-vailing trends. The peace movement for example has grown in strength despite official propaganda and the riots and the Scarman report and subsequent debates have highlighted failings in the police and perhaps marked the beginnings of collapse in articulated public confidence in the police. The trend towards the state management of the nation is not inexorable, and it will not go unchallenged.

And now the news

Our image of the social order is partly derived from the information received from the mass media. This information comes in many forms: implicitly in novels, drama, etc. and explicitly in the coverage of contemporary events. I will concentrate on the latter.

The state has an important role to play in the coverage of news. In the first place it provides the legislative context in which the newspapers, television and radio operate. The legal framework sets the limits within which the media conducts its business. With newspapers, the degree of official direct control is less than that of television and radio. Newspapers are owned in Britain by major corporations (although the *Guardian* is owned by a non-profit-making trust) and ultimate control rests with powerful private interests. There are three sectors of the newspaper market: the mass circulation end taken up by the *Sun, Mirror* and *Star*; the middle-order group of the *Mail* and the *Express* and the so-called quality press including the *Telegraph, Guardian* and *The Times*. Apart from the *Guardian* and the *Mirror* the newspapers tend to support the Conservative party and the range of political dialogue opened up by the newspapers is limited. The demise of the *Herald* in the 1960s marked the end of a serious mass newspaper which recognised the validity of a socialist alternative and was aware of a liberal tradition. The *Herald* was the victim of newspaper economics because even with a circulation of a million copies it was unable to survive. There is little doubt that the mass of both serious and popular newspapers are pro-Conservative, anti-Labour, anti-socialist and represent and articulate capital interests. What is the question is whether this organised opinion has any effect on political attitudes and dispositions. People have voted Labour despite the newspapers, in large measure newspapers tend to speak to the converted.

What is of equal or greater importance has been the rise of television to its role of being the main source of public information in our society. The main news bulletins of ITV and BBC are watched by almost sixteen million viewers. Unlike the newspapers, television is widely held to be an important source of impartial information. Here state control is more evident. The BBC obtains its charter from the government, its fees are collected by the government and like the IBA the controlling bodies are government appointed. In everyday operations there is little direct government intervention but government controls exist and have been used. During the Falklands war for example the television news was in a large measure a channel for official government propaganda.

The mass media rely on the state for information. There is a degree of symbiosis between the government and the media, although criticisms are made by either side as Whale (1977) has noted:

> . . . it would be wrong to represent journalism and Government as adversaries and nothing else. At the least they are adversaries who depend on one another like professional wrestlers endlessly renewing the same bout in different rings. Government needs journalists in order to have its deeds and expectations publicly set out. Journalism, anxious to make the world as interesting and comprehensible as possible, constantly asks the Government machine for help – information from the Ministry press office, an interview with the Minister himself . . . The mutual dependence is there . . . it is especially true of broadcasters. (p. 122)

The media represent the views of the government often

directly as in the lobby system where accredited journalist feed off the government press officers and more indirectly by giving preferential access to the media to government spokesmen. If there was a clear and unequivocal relationship between the mass of opinion, real events, government opinion and television representation there would be little cause for complaint or worry. When the television news reports the consensus there is little tension or potential conflict. The problem arises because in some cases opinions have differed, alternative explanations of events exist and the relationship between the government and the governed is not always harmonious. But the television news seems incapable of handling tensions. In an important series of books, the Glasgow University Media Group (GUMG, 1977, 1980) have argued that television news reporting gives a partial view of the world and in so doing invalidates the professed claim of fairness and objectivity. The starting-point for media news coverage is an acceptance of the principle of private ownership, normal workings of the private market and the main elements which make up the status quo. It is a view of society in harmony, of a nation with a broad base of consensus. From this perspective how has the television news covered the collapse of post-war consensus associated with the beginnings of economic decline? The GUMG have highlighted three aspects. First, they show how in most coverage of industrial relations strikes are depicted as disruptions to normal production and implicit blame is placed on workers. More generally, industrial ills are related to problems of labour discipline rather than lack of investment or management incompetence. The search is made in the media for both disruptive elements and the negative consequences of strike action. Second, in economic coverage especially during the 1970s the GUMG show how news was organised around demonstrating the link between wages and inflation. Wage increases were seen as the cause of inflation and the rightness of a wage policy was implicitly as well as explicitly demonstrated. Third, the treatment of news was also biased against political alternatives:

The news is profoundly committed to a distinct social and political order. The preferential treatment accorded to some right-wingers is only part of this. A second critical feature is the closing off of possible alternatives. Information which contradicts the preferred view or which would give credibility to the alternatives, is either rewritten, downgraded or simply left out. The attempts to democratise the Labour Party are presented as if they are themselves undemocratic. The 'pressure' from below is to be closed off and a favourite theme of media coverage becomes the question of how democratic is the Labour Party at its base? Who is pulling the strings? (Philo *et al.*, 1982, pp. 88–9)

We may also add that the media coverage of crime has strengthened the shift to the authoritarian society, amplifying the arguments of the law and order brigade, and in the coverage of race the media has only dealt with race issues when they become problems thus making the link between ethnic minority and social malaise.

This bias has been achieved through:

(1) *The use of language.* Workers 'demand' wage increases, 'threaten' strike action and 'disrupt' production while management make 'offers' and 'plead' for a return to work. Similarly existing government policies are seen as realistic and sober while reflationary policies are 'wasteful' and 'spendthrift'. In its coverage of politics Left-wing views are clearly associated with 'trouble' and 'domination' to be compared with 'moderate' and 'compromises'. The language of the news is the language of bias.

(2) *Differential access to the media.* Senior politicians, 'responsible' union leaders and government spokesmen are regularly consulted and their views given a high order in the presentation of explanations. The ideology of the status quo is drip-fed through the news by regular coverage of establishment views and thoughts. Greater access to the news is given to the strong and powerful. The GUMG show how in a television news coverage of a dustcart drivers' strike in Glasgow, when there were over fourteen bulletins and ten people were interviewed a total of twenty-one times, not one striker was interviewed. Equality of access to the media is a prerequisite of an impartial news service.

(3) *The structuring of the news.* The news is covered so that only one set of explanations is given good coverage. In terms of industrial relations the whole angle of news coverage is from the point of view that strikers cause problems and strikes themselves are a prime cause of economic decline. Information which promotes alternative explanations, such as poor investment performance, are either ignored, downgraded or presented as irrational fragments. Alternative opinions are given access it is true but in a context which shows them to be unrealistic, irrational and against the self-evident natural logic of things:

> The context of the news is organised in such a way that coherence is given to only one set of explanations and policies. What we are indicating here is not isolated pieces of 'bias'. The problem is much more profound than this. The logic of one group of explanations is built into the text. This logic dictates the flow of information, the range of accounts and the legitimacy that is given to these. (Philo *et al.*, 1982, p. 59)

There is little direct state control over television news coverage because there is little need for it. As John Whale has noted the BBC has preserved its independence by testing it as seldom as possible. The news coverage, however, is not a completely closed system. There are two sources of change. First, change from the top. This has arisen recently because the 1979 Conservative government signalled an end or at least a change to the post-war political consensus between the major political parties, including the lack of commitment to full employment and welfare services, the belief in the importance of inflation as opposed to unemployment and the belief in the control of the money supply rather than wage increases to halt inflation have all provoked a change in standard government pronouncements. Television news coverage has been placed in an ambiguous position between representing the views of the government on the one hand yet having a commitment to the politics and a view of a consensual society which lies mid-way between the Right of the Labour party and the Left of the

Conservative party. It operates uncomfortably with the new Right in the Conservative party and the emerging Left in the Labour party. Second, 'there is change from below. Public sector strikes, the rise of the Campaign for Nuclear Disarmament (CND) and the development of political alternatives have arisen despite the media. Apart from the SDP which in a sense is a creation of the media, these alternatives have not been given access to the news service. Thus strikes are still covered from the angle of disruption; pictures of huge CND rallies are counterbalanced by providing ready platforms for defence spokesmen and coverage of the Left wing of the Labour party is regularly associated with the rise of militancy. In the long term these alternatives can and may grow but in the short and medium term any alternatives to the existing bedrock of government policies has to fight against unfavourable television coverage.

At the local level there is a similar symbiosis between the media and the local authorities. The largest local newspapers are privately-owned and generally by the same corporations which own national newspapers. Their reliance on the local authority and their commitment to private interests guide their coverage of local events. The local media are often unwilling to articulate popular demands from the governed to the government especially if this raises fundamental challenges to the local authorities but local media forms a well-worn channel of communication from local government to the governed.

In order to maintain its audience, television news has to capture popular opinion. The newspapers in contrast concentrate on segments of the population, repeating and amplifying the readers' opinions and prejudice. In large part the media makes this opinion but in order to maintain credibility it must also relate to it. We can see something of this in the coverage of unemployment. In periods of low unemployment especially during the 1960s and very early 1970s the unemployed were seen as shifty and work-shy layabouts scrounging on the generous welfare state. This was the popular opinion amplified in the media. As unemployment began to rise the scrounger theme continued but took on less credibility as a convincing explanation. Not all three and a half million people could be seen as scroungers. The work-shy theme did not disappear but added to it were other more structural factors, not all of them sympathetic. One emerging explanation advanced by various government spokesmen was the notion that workers were pricing themselves out of a job. However, the media was beginning to shift, albeit slowly, as a function of the reality of the situation. In that sense the television' news coverage does have to bear some resemblance to reality but the reality it presents is partial. The steady drip of official pronouncements, establishment values and status quo apologetics are carried by the channels of mass communication. And they have an effect. They limit the range of policy alternatives and close off avenues of discussion. The range of policy solutions is restricted to a carefully selected few. In its coverage of contemporary events the news media not only reports action but constrains it.

The state and crises

We can best summarise the main findings of this and the previous chapter as a series of comments on the crises identified in Figure 2.5 on page 25.

A crisis of legitimation?

In mainland Britain there has not been a wholesale loss of public confidence in the state apparatus but the two major political parties have lost support and their remaining support has been polarised into different parts of the country. Tory voters are concentrated in suburban and Shire counties while Labour maintains a level of support in the cities and the older industrial areas. This polarised pattern is part cause and part effect of the divergence in party policies. Tory governments can now pursue a free market policy more easily if the areas most badly affected are unlikely to return Conservatives.

Apart from Northern Ireland there has been no substantial loss of mass loyalty endangering the orderly reproduction of social political life, but there has been the revolt of the young blacks in the inner cities who have been marginalised by society. The riots of 1981 were, in Scarman's words, 'a burst of anger' against coercive policing, limited employment prospects and deteriorating life chances. This form of social movement is unlikely to be replicated in other parts of the country combining as it did youth alienation, racism, police incompetence and a whole host of contingent factors. However, the events did indicate one reaction of a black youth underclass in a declining economy. The main crisis of legitimation for the British state has been in the communities of Northern Ireland.

A fiscal crisis?

A fiscal crisis occurs when expenditure outruns revenue. In Britain the crisis has been partly solved by increasing and widening the taxation load. Even the Conservative government which came to power in 1979 strongly committed to tax cuts had to admit in 1982 that average wage-earners were paying more tax. But even with a wide and deep tax base expenditure has outrun revenue. To close the gap between getting and spending, spending cuts have been attempted. These have been greatest in welfare-type expenditure affecting those already most affected by the recession. Attempts at reducing government spending have involved strained relations between central and local governments especially between central Conservative governments and high-spending Labour local governments. The early 1980s saw the imposition of greater central control on local government spending. The use of cash limits to cap expenditure has as its main consequence a growing confrontation between public service unions on the one hand seeking wage increases and government and quasi-government bodies on the other seeking to limit expenditure. The fiscal crisis has not been so much a failure to meet expenditure but the redistributional consequences of controlling and redirecting expenditure.

Rationality crises?

Type 1. From 1951 until the mid 1960s the general role of the state in the economic sphere was not a matter of serious debate.

Both major political parties accepted, albeit to varying degrees, the principles of Keynesian demand management. Unemployment was reduced by the reflation of increased public expenditure and encouragement to private spending while inflation was reduced by such deflationary measures as credit restrictions. With the ending of the long boom, and as downturn in the world economy turned into a sustained recession, the general role of the state once again became a subject for serious debate in Britain. The early years of the Heath government in 1970 and the Thatcher government of 1979 showed an emerging Right-wing perspective, one which stressed sound money, the need to combat the power of the trade unions and a firm belief in the efficacy of market forces. A growing Conservative school of thought, best articulated by Sir Keith Joseph, argued that present and future Conservative governments had to shift to the Right. The post-war years had seen growing statism and a steady drift to the Left. If Conservatives came to office without radical policies they would be dragged Leftwards. The Tories, so it was argued, had to be radical in order to regain the middle ground of British politics. In economic matters the Conservative's philosophy could best be summed up in the phrase, 'return to market forces'.

There was also a radicalising of the Labour party. The experience of rising unemployment, the failures of the Wilson–Callaghan governments and the performance of the 1979 Thatcher government all left their mark. The Labour party of the early 1980s was beginning to evolve an alternative economic strategy based on import controls, planning agreements and the democratisation of the workplace. These were all far cries from the white heat of technology proposed in the mid 1960s.

One effect of the crisis then was to provoke different answers for its solution. Each proposed solution (or set of solutions to be more accurate) had to meet different sets of problems. The free market solution first attempted by Heath was abandoned in the face of growing unemployment. The 1979 Conservative government showed more resolve but at a price. Increasing unemployment led to a polarisation of political support: even with three and a half million unemployed the majority of the working population was still in employment, most of them experiencing small increases in standards of living, and there were whole areas of the country especially in the exurban and suburban districts where the recession had less impact, inflation-orientated strategies were appreciated and Conservatives could continue to count on support. The converse was a worsening situation in inner urban areas and the older industrial centres. However, if the Conservatives continue to restructure Britain along the contours of a private market economy then they will continue to meet resistance from organised labour.

The main problem of the Labour party will be to get elected. Loss of support has placed them in a difficult electoral position unlikely to win outright with a large enough majority to carry through their radical reforms. Even assuming that they could achieve a parliamentary victory in the future then they would come up against the power of capital, the city and entrenched bureaucracies. The experience of Mitterrand's France shows the difficulties of pursuing a reflationary policy with the world economy in recession.

Type 2. The state's role in reproducing the social order is a complex one. It is clear that there is no such thing as a simple rationality crisis but a whole series of varied and overlapping tensions. The state is the scene of struggle for those wishing to restructure the different elements of the state apparatus. Although the issues vary in detail by the different sectors, the generalities of limited expenditure and conflicting opinions remain constant. The end of the post-war consensus is being articulated in debates about education, law and order, the health service and the myriad of issues and realms in which the state is involved. The crisis of rationality is not so much a question of not knowing what to do but a conflict between sharply differing opinions of the form and nature of state social policies. The conflict has sharpened because the different solutions have marked redistributional consequences.

5

Community Concerns

Community concerns are expressed by people as residents, as users and consumers of particular places, through community groups, amenity societies, residents' associations and tenants' organisations (I will use the terms interchangeably throughout this chapter). They are concerns with places as *living places*, to be contrasted and distinguished from the concerns of capital with places as markets, sources of profit and scenes for economic calculation and the concerns of the state with places populated by people as voters. The concept of community is clearly problematic. It has been used to refer to the small-scale to be contrasted with mass society, to informal relationships to be compared with 'unnatural' anonymous relationships. The term has all sorts of ideological connotations. In this chapter I will refer to 'community concerns' as essentially small-scale, localised action, whose organisations operate both inside and outside formal channels of representation. These concerns are worthy of consideration because they are of growing importance. Community concerns highlight and articulate some of the relationships between the state and the population, and the links between capital and the state in specific places have been mediated by community action. Community, then, along with capital and the state provides a major element in the analysis of contemporary British society.

The context

Community organisations have been growing in size and importance. Figure 5.1, for example, shows the increase in the number of amenity societies throughout the 1960s and 1970s. As Barker (1976) notes:

> the 'local amenity movement' in Britain is a wide ranging, diverse and overlapping collection of local voluntary groups

126

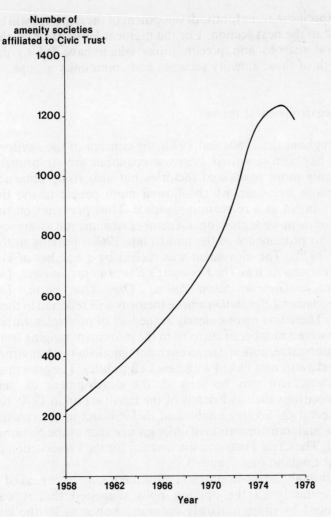

Number of amenity societies affiliated to Civic Trust

FIGURE 5.1 *The growth of amenity societies*

who seek to take an interest in some aspect of their home surroundings, their neighbourhood, village, town or area. . . . Those who have joined a 'community action' group or a residents association of some kind have done so in the hope of improving their lot by public political pressure on the authorities. (p. 7)

The specific reasons for the development of these groups will be noted in the next section. For the moment let us examine the general reasons and preconditions which have led to the growth of these amenity societies and community groups.

The environmental theme

Throughout the 1960s and 1970s the concept of the environment has been sensitised. Post-war economic growth brought not only more roads and factories but also rising affluence and more free time, which allowed more people to use the environment as a recreation resource. Thus pressures on the environment were growing. General environmental awareness came to prominence in the mid to late 1960s, peaking in the early 1970s. The movement was fuelled by a number of key publications such as *The Ecologist's Blueprint for Survival, The Limits to Growth, Silent Spring, Only One Earth, The Environmental Revolution* whose theme is well reflected in their titles. There was no one clearly argued set of principles, rather there were a number of currents in the movement ranging from a conservative, authoritarian environmentalism to an environmental awareness linked with new Left politics. The growth of the movement can be seen in the development of new organisations such as Friends of the Earth set up in 1970, the Conservation Society established in 1967 and in the resuscitation and transformation of older groups such as the National Trust, The Civic Trust and the Council for the Preservation of Rural England (see Figure 5.2).

Although the environmental movement may have peaked – and certainly all the opinion polls suggested that it was displaced by more narrowly economic concerns by the late 1970s – it has nevertheless left as legacy a number of important pressure groups, and a public awareness of environmental issues. The environmental movement became so popular partly because it allowed people to couple, at least in their own minds, local interests with global responsibilities. As part of our contemporary cultural language, the idiom of environmentalism has allowed local groups to fuse local issues with world concerns and their own interests with 'scientific rationality' and

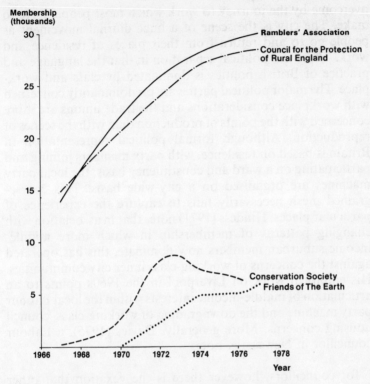

FIGURE 5.2 *The growth of environmental groups*

'global humanism'. By appealing to and using the notion of 'environment', local groups have been able to gain greater purchase for their own goals while their local concerns have been informed by larger debates. The environmental movement has both informed and stimulated the growth of community groups.

Home—workplace separation

One of the fundamental characteristics of British cities is the separation between residence and workplace: separation in a number of senses. There is a physical separation which is only overcome by the journey to work which most people have to make. The city is the scene of a huge diurnal movement as people go to and return from their places of residence and work. There is a political separation in that the language and practice of British politics is dominated by class and work-place. The major political parties are predominantly concerned with workplace considerations and the trade unions are more concerned with the points of production than with the scenes of reproduction. Although formal political representation in Britain is based on residence, with party members joining and participating on a ward and constituency basis, the local party machines are organised on a city-wide basis. This coarse-grained mesh necessarily fails to capture the experience of particular places. Hindess (1971) notes that in association with changing patterns of membership in which more middle-income suburban members now dominate, this has operated against the concerns of working-class inner city communities. His empirical work on Liverpool in the 1960s points to an articulation of middle-income interests within the local Labour party machine and the downgrading of working-class, council housing concerns. More generally, Davies (1975), a Labour councillor in Newcastle, notes:

for councillors, however there is the vexation that other demands of their role make it unlikely that they can be as 'ward-specific' in their knowledge and responses as can an activist . . . . Most County Borough Councillors are mem-bers of political parties and very often the 'party line', the party record and party loyalties make it very costly and perhaps impossible to respond to Ward interests when those interests are in conflict with party policy.

For party councillors times are particularly trying when one's party is in power for then, added to the constraint of the 'party line' (which puts a block on public criticism of the Council) there are the whole range of subtle (and not so subtle) pressures and invitations to act as the front-man for political colleagues and officials. The councillor who per-sistently acts as an ombudsman for his Ward very soon provokes irritation and is simply frozen out of all the patterns of information-flow and the perpetual 'brokerage' that constitutes the political aspect of local government. (p. 84)

This relationship between councillor and areal representation varies. In more marginal seats councillors may be more receptive to local opinion as their political survival may depend on their responsiveness. It also varies by political party. Local Liberal councillors have been less restrained by their local political machine. The involvement of Liberals in local government in the late 1960s was associated with the growing language and practice of community politics. This may change however as Liberals move from being a small third party to a major political force. We may then have to revise Davies's following comments:

to date at any rate Liberal candidates in local elections have been effectively free of party constraints and have been able like activists, to put 'community politics' first, hence the resentment we 'party hacks' have for liberal candidates who seem to have the advantages of a party label without any of the disadvantages. (p. 84)

In general then the local authorities are effectively insulated from electoral influences at a place-specific level. As Dunleavy (1980) notes:

the debate and arguments in local authorities can largely be interpreted in terms of a small number of local government ideologies expressing the general interests and orientations of particular intra-institutional positions or organisational situations, rather than reflecting specifically local area- or 'community'-orientated responses to policy problems. (p. 160)

The failure of the formal political channels to either represent or articulate place-specific issues has provided the rationale for the rise of community groups. This precondition has been activated by changes in the housing market and the politicisation of community issues.

The housing market

The most important changes in the housing market in Britain has been the rise of owner-occupation, the increase in local authority renting and the decline of the private rented sector. These changes have had profound effects.

The increase in owner-occupation has been a continuing feature of housing in twentieth-century Britain. In 1914 less than one in ten households were owner-occupiers but by 1945 one in four and by 1980 one in two. Owner-occupation, unlike the other two tenure types, provides not only shelter but also an opportunity for monetary gain. If owner-occupiers sell their housing for more than they paid they have made a notional profit. This is a real profit if the rate of return is greater than the rate of inflation. In post-war Britain most owner-occupiers have had a steadily appreciating asset and housing has been one of the most profitable forms of investment, one aided by tax relief on mortgage repayments and the ability to pocket gains from selling a house without paying capital gains tax (see Short, 1982b). Owner-occupation has been a source of wealth as well as a form of accommodation.

The value of an owner-occupier's dwelling partly derives from the internal nature of the dwelling, i.e. size, age, quality, etc. and partly from the nature of the external environment. There are certain external aspects which increase and decrease the value of housing, these are termed respectively positive and negative externalities. The construction of a motorway can be termed a negative externality for the neighbourhoods that it passes through as it is likely to depress the value of the housing while the improvement of a public building is likely to be a positive externality in so far as it increases the overall attractiveness of the area. These externalities vary in space. A motorway for example may be a positive externality for distant suburbanites enabling them to travel to work, so that values in distant suburban areas may therefore be increased, whereas at the more local level the motorway would be a negative externality for residential areas on either side of the route. These variations in space thus mean that externalities affect different groups of people in different locations.

Much resident group activity arises from owner-occupiers

seeking to band together to protect and enhance their property values. The rise of owner-occupation has given a material basis for much community action.

In council housing the local authority is the landlord. Much council housing, especially in urban areas, is in the form of large estates with similar housing types and layout. Tenants on these estates have a shared housing experience and a common landlord, something which rarely occurs in private renting. This precondition of community action has been activated by a number of factors. Much of the post-1960 council housing in urban areas took the form of high-rise flats which were unpopular, difficult and expensive to heat, and often with severe problems of damp and condensation. The municipal housing utopias of the 1960s have become the vandalised dumps of the 1980s. Dissatisfaction over housing provision, in association with discontent over rising rents, provided the basis for mobilisation in council housing estates. Community action was not the only response, of course, since those households who could afford to do so left the council house sector to join the swelling ranks of owner-occupiers, and many of those who remained sought to move to the better-quality council housing in the more favoured estates. But in some estates residents have been sufficiently aggrieved to mobilise support for community action, ranging from lobbying of councillors, demonstrations to rent strikes. The pages of the journal *Community Action* tell a story of rising mobilisation throughout the 1970s.

Community concerns and the women's movement

The rise of community action also owes a lot to the development of feminism as a political force and the growth of the women's movement. It is women in the main who have shouldered the responsibilities of home and children. They have a more direct interest and experience of community matters such as schooling, levels of local public service provision, access to housing, levels of local traffic flows, etc. Sometimes the relationship between feminism and community involvement was direct and explicit. Lynne Segal, for example, describes the setting up of a local group and community newspaper which sought to make links between the subjective experience of women and wider community matters (Rowbotham *et al.*, 1979). More common was a more implicit, more partial and gradual realisation of the relationships between the experience of women in the family, the home and the community through small-scale, local organisations. There has been a reciprocal relationship. Much of community action has involved women while some of the consciousness-raising of women has been because of and through community action. Much of the strength of community action has come from women while some of the new found confidence within the women's movement has come through community action.

The state, politicisation and the crisis of consumption

We have seen in the previous chapter how the role of the state has increased enormously. The state now provides transport, housing, health services, social services and the bulk of education. The shift from market to state provision is more than just a change in the identity of the provider. It provides a change in the whole nature of provision. What was previously the subject of narrowly economic criteria now becomes involved in questions of equity and fiscal responsibility through political bargaining and compromise. The entry of the state politicises a whole range of urban public services as provision of these services becomes the very stuff of domestic politics. Financial considerations are still important but they are now tempered by wider political issues. This politicisation takes a number of forms. It allows users as electors to wield some form of political power. While the pure free market responds only to economic power, the public market also reacts to political power. By its nature therefore the provision of urban public goods and services allows the meaningful representation of users' interests. Indeed the fact of politicisation encourages representation as some elected representatives seek to maintain their power base and represent interests on an organised basis. There are tensions between the different interests involved.

On the one hand there are limits to public expenditure on welfare provision. In a recession these limits are more tightly drawn, as the state finds it increasingly difficult to increase its revenue base since both corporate and private tax-payers are victims of economic contraction, while certain business interests even seek to redirect state expenditure. On the other hand there are demands made by groups of consumers, the most powerful being business interests and articulate, middle-income groups, and public service unions who want more investment and higher wages. The precise balance of forces varies over time and from case to case. But the general tendency in recent years has been for demands to increase while the political response to the current recession has been to entail greater limits being placed on public expenditure. While the demand for urban public services has increased the ability to pay for them has been curtailed. Several consequences have followed. Some people, and particularly the richer ones, have opted out of the public sector by turning to private health systems or sending their children to private (so-called 'public') schools; others have revised their expectations downwards, while still others have come together in groups to resist the decline in services by taking some form of direct action. Parents have demonstrated outside schools due for closure, and commuters have refused to pay for increased fares. These urban struggles constitute a form of consumer trade unionism.

Pressure from below, stimulation from above

The development of community groups and community action has also risen from wider political initiatives. Three types can be identified. The first is what we may term the 'grass-roots movement', which sought to radicalise people through community action. The community activists, mainly operating in inner city areas, included Liberals and socialists seeking to forge links between the politics of workplace and residence. Throughout the 1960s and 1970s community workers were active with varying degrees of success in radicalising residents. Action-research schemes from local colleges and universities, local politicians and radicalised state workers provided the base for much of this activity. Second, recent years have also seen the growth of state attempts to incorporate community action, in order to avoid further confrontation, to minimise costly political errors, to obtain information and to legitimate existing and future action. This complex set of factors can be summarily described as 'public participation'. Beginning with the Skeffington report in 1969, which called for greater public participation in planning, there have been a series of public participation schemes ranging from structure plan preparations, the use of neighbourhood councils to the Community Development Projects (CDP, 1977a,b). These various schemes have been criticised by many who see them simply as means of securing legitimation in the face of declining public services provision, dwindling budgets and sharpening conflict between competing interests. To a very large extent this is true: certainly many of the participation exercises in land use planning and structure plan preparation have sought to justify the official line. But this critique ignores the opportunities afforded by participation schemes, which do open some issues for public debate. Simply to write them off is to ignore the political openings which these schemes create. In her analysis of Lambeth, for example, Cockburn (1977) showed that while some of the neighbourhood councils did indeed simply legitimate official council policy, they also became involved with local squatting movements and called council housing policy into question. Part of the problem lies with the use of the word 'participation' itself. It covers a variety of experiences. Arnstein (1971) provides a useful starting point in a more careful conceptualisation, shown in Figure 5.3, and suggests a ladder of citizen participation. At the bottom is non-participation, in which residents are simply manipulated or their problems are seen to lie in themselves. Much of the initial CDP programmes for example was based on a culture of poverty thesis which saw poverty as being due to the characteristics of the poor; the solutions were thus seen in terms of individual improvement. Then there are varieties of tokenism, ranging from the authorities simply informing the population to a form of placation. Even the exercise of public power can range from delegation to public control. Most public participation schemes fall within the area of tokenism identified by

Degrees of
public power
{
Public control
Delegated power
Partnership: sharing power

Tokenism
{
Placation
Consultation: inviting opinion
Informing

Manipulation
{
Therapy: focus on individual pathology, manipulation (rubber stamp)

FIGURE 5.3   *A ladder of participation*

SOURCE: Arnstein, S. R. (1971) 'A ladder of citizen participation in the USA', *Journal of Town Planning Institute*, vol. 57, pp. 176–82.

Arnstein, but in its fuller sense public participation should mean public control.

Finally there have not only been bottom-up ('grass-roots') and top-down ('tokenism') political initiatives; one of the most important types has been what we might call 'middle-up'. Occupational and educational changes in post-war Britain have produced congeries of articulate middle-income groups. This growing middle class, predominantly owner-occupiers and thus with an important material interest, has provided the basis for much resident group and amenity group activity. Rich enough to be able to afford their own house or flat, but not rich enough to escape completely from the city's externality surface, say by moving to an exclusive, green-belt village protected by the whole gamut of planning controls, they are a vulnerable group who can articulate their concerns. Public participation in contemporary Britain has been more of a middle-up phenomena than a bottom-up process.

These three kinds of initiatives are not independent. The state has introduced public participation schemes in order to harness the rise of grass-roots movements, and many community groups of the middle-up type have been formed in response to the institutional openings created by public participation schemes. This interdependence is apparent at the individual level as community workers employed by the state can become agents of consciousness-raising in local neighbour-hoods and prime movers of community action. The whole CDP experiment provides a classic example of a state initiative creating a group of workers who transformed the scheme into a more radical critique of official policy and practice (CDP, 1977a). Participation schemes, community organisations and community action have become the main terrain for top-down and bottom-up political initiatives.

General observations

Between the preconditions for community groups and the creation of such groups lies the mobilisation of opinion. There are a number of general principles which have been enunciated for describing the process of community group creation. Groups are formed either through promotional efforts by outside agencies – for example, local authorities, action research groups, etc. and/or the perception by potential members that important issues can be solved or affected by collective action. This implies that there are people who have the time, commitment and belief to secure mobilisation of local opinion. And often community groups wax and wane as more active individuals enter and leave particular areas and spheres of local public life. Most community groups start up through the actions of a few or often only one individual, and in the early stages community groups tend to have a very definite core–periphery structure to their membership. A small active core group provides the bulk of labour input and commitment, with the wider membership being peripheral to decision-making, goal-setting and the day-to-day running of the group. Two broad types of strategies are adopted by most community groups. *Service* strategies are concerned to use and mobilise the community's own resources, either through complementary strategies (augmenting existing service provision), alternative strategies (trying to demonstrate a new way of meeting a need and providing an alternative) and/or substitute strategies (in an attempt to replace existing forms of service provision). *Influence* strategies involve the deflection of externalities and resource provision and allocation to the area or group of people represented by the community group. Three separate influence strategies can be identified:

(1) Collaborative strategies in which there is a shared set of basic assumptions between the authority and the group.
(2) Campaign strategies where the community group seeks to demonstrate the need for additional resources.
(3) Coercive strategies in which the group seeks to or has to confront the authorities (see Figure 5.4).

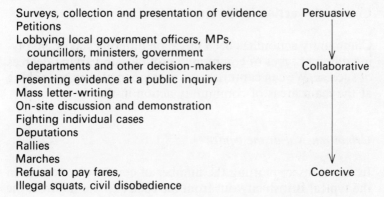

FIGURE 5.4 *The continuum of influence strategies*

In this chapter I am most concerned with influence strategies. The relative success of community groups' influence campaigns depends on a number of factors, the most important being the organisational experience, skills and commitment of core group members. From this organisational base, community group success depends upon not only the ability of the group to mobilise and maintain support, mount effective campaigns and choose the most effective strategies, but also the degree of receptivity of the group to the authorities. The most effective campaigns of small-scale community groups will fail if central government or local authority is vehemently opposed to them. On the other hand even a poorly organised community group strategy may be successful if the relevant authorities are – for whatever reason – keen to meet their demands.

The effects of the rise of community concerns and community action can be examined in a number of ways. In the next section I will seek to show the main scenes of community action in the city and to identify their major effects. I will then reconsider some of this material by examining the general relationships between community, capital and the state. The aim of this final section will be not only to summarise past relationships but to indicate the course of future ones.

Community action in the city

Community action has been based on differing stakes, involving different types of community groups with varying degrees of success. We can capture some of this complexity by looking at the main areas of community action in the city.

Urban renewal at the centre

In any transect plotting the number of community actions in the typical British city out from the centre to the suburbs, the residential area bordering the commercial core of the city centre would loom large. A useful analogy can be derived from the notion of plate tectonics, which sees the world's geological surface as composed of a number of large plates. Volcanic activity rarely occurs within plates but generally at the edges where plates shunt and bump together. It is much the same within the city, where the plates of residential areas collide with the plates of commercial and industrial land uses. The communities bordering the city centre have been affected by two interlinked processes. The first was the clearance and rebuilding schemes of local authorities. From the mid 1950s through to the mid 1970s national housing policy concerning older property was one of comprehensive redevelopment: knock down old houses and build new ones. Municipal bulldozers swept through much of inner city Britain, clearing housing and flattening long-established residential areas. The rebuilding took a number of forms, but the predominant models were of high-rise blocks in the inner areas and lower density estates in more suburban areas. This form of urban renewal clearly involved community disruption. Community response in the early years was notable by its absence. Much of the renewal was taking place in closely-knit, working-class communities which had strong internal associations but which often lacked the resources and the confidence to protest effectively. Some community groups did emerge, but their protests were either blocked or so disorganised that they petered out. For the most part they were involved in an unequal struggle with the local authorities. In his case study of Beckton in the London borough of Newham, for example, Dunleavy (1977) paints a picture of a weak, poorly-organised community group failing to achieve any influence on a local authority which did not acknowledge the legitimacy or even the existence of the protest movement. The variations in resources and constraints of the protagonists are shown in Table 5.1. As Dunleavy notes:

the Beckton residents failed to produce a change in their housing. Their movement had no leverage on the power of the public housing apparatus and it could not gain any in the face of repressive responses. Even if the protestors had influenced decision-making they would not have done so because they forced the authority to take notice of them, but because actors in the authority were willing to be influenced. The fact that these actors *did not want to be influenced* is indicative of the strength of the structural forces tying the locality into the general development of public housing policy. The basic tendency of this development, towards the reproduction of an unequal status quo with the inner city working class at the bottom of the pile, was far too strongly entrenched to be capable of alteration either by the protest movement or by the local authority. (p. 215, emphasis in original)

Things began to change in some areas by the late 1960s. There was a change in government policy away from redevelopment towards less expensive improvement and rehabilitation schemes. This revised housing policy emerged from the 1967–8 devaluation of the pound and the central government's

142

TABLE 5.1   *An unequal struggle*

Power resources	Constraints
Local authorities	
Monopoly of information, decision and timing	Reference public opinion
Minimisation or withdrawal of services	
Blight creation: neglect of repairs	
Withholding of payments related to Compulsory Purchase Orders	
Creation of neighbourhood conflicts	
Control of jobs (of employees of council and businesses displaced by clearance)	
Unfavourable typing of residents	
Unfavourable housing allocations	
Withdrawal of housing rights	
Eviction	
Clearance area residents	
Access to councillors	Uncertainty, lack of information
Access to local media	Poor conditions (therefore high costs of delay)
Access to reference publics	Dispersion (in many cases)
Direct action	Virtually complete housing vulnerability
	Job vulnerability (of local authority employees and employees of businesses displaced by clearance)

SOURCE: Dunleavy, P. (1977) 'Protest and Quiescence in Urban Politics: A Critique of some Pluralist and Structuralist Myths', *International Journal of Urban and Regional Research*, vol. 1, pp. 193–218.

decision to cut public expenditure in its wake. Public housing policies were now fashioned on smaller budgets. But there was also stiffening resistance at the local level. The worst housing areas had been cleared in the first waves, so that the municipal bulldozer was now facing better housing areas, where arguments for clearance were less compelling. Clearance schemes were now coming up against more affluent, more articulate, better-organised communities, who provided more effective resistance against the local authorities. The later clearance schemes were also occurring after the introduction of public participation exercises, which provided an institutional opening and an organisational base for community group protests. Consider the following example from the city of Bristol. There, in 1972, Labour gained control of the city council in the local elections and immediately began to initiate and consider plans for urban renewal in certain inner city areas, including St Paul's. As a preliminary to redevelopment the Housing Committee instructed that no further improvement grants should be given in St Paul's and that a survey of housing conditions in the area was to be conducted by the Public Health Department. In 1973 the Housing Department suggested that compulsory purchase orders should be used and a comprehensive redevelopment scheme followed. The chief of the Housing Department rejected a policy of improvement, that is keeping existing houses and improving them *in situ*, on a number of grounds. Clearance was the only way to ensure that the dwellings were brought up to proper standards, he argued, and satisfactory traffic layouts could be improved while previous evidence suggested that voluntary improvement schemes could not be relied upon. A timetable was drawn up – a public meeting in July 1974 to discuss the proposals, the compulsory purchase orders to be confirmed by December 1975 and construction to begin in 1976. But this timetable of events was never achieved. At the public meeting residents objected that inadequate compensation would be offered and that the community would be broken up. These objections were raised primarily by a pressure group originally formed to combat motorway proposals, consisting of middle-class households living in adjacent areas. The voice of the poorest residents, those renting their homes in the private sector, was not heard at the meeting. The central authorities also began to put pressure on the local authority. The Department of the Environment, reflecting the national policy swing to improvement, let it be known that the permission of the Secretary of State for compulsory purchase orders would not be forthcoming. Under this dual pressure the redevelopment proposals were dropped and the second housing report of November 1974 suggested an improvement programme (see Short and Bassett, 1981). In this example we can see a tie-up between certain community interests and central government, and more generally we can say that the pendulum of housing policy has now swung away from comprehensive redevelopment to improvement partly through community pressure but mainly because of central government directives. In other words, community concerns have been successful in recent years in stopping the municipal bulldozer because they have coincided with the wishes of central government.

The second process affecting some inner city communities has been the commercial redevelopment of central and inner city sites. This is a continual process: as vacant sites are developed, existing sites are demolished and refurbished, all as part of an attempt to make money out of property development. The financial logic behind these schemes is clear; Table 5.2 shows the return from different types of land use. It is clear that most owners and developers have a clear incentive to change the use of their property in order to maximise their return. Although occurring all the time to a certain extent, in post-war Britain there have been two main waves of property development. The first was in the period from 1958 to the mid 1960s, when there was a commercial boom associated with the construction of major shopping and office complexes in the large and medium cities. This was often aided and encouraged by local authorities eager to show a modernised city image and gain from the increase in rateable values. At this stage community protests were either lacking, or muted and unable to achieve political leverage. The redevelopment schemes went ahead largely untouched by local community concerns. The second wave occurred in the early to mid 1970s and this time the dominant theme of the property boom was office construction. The boom was driven by demand for office space and

TABLE 5.2   *The relationship between land use and revenue in British cities*

Land use	Gross annual revenue over 1,000 sq. ft of site* (£)
Housing (private renting)	400
Factories/warehouses	1,000
Shops	3,000
Offices (provincial cities)	16,000
Offices (central London)	60,000

*Including allowances for differences in plot ratio.

SOURCE: Ambrose (1976).

lubricated by investment from banks and other financial institutions (see Chapter 3 and Figure 3.7). This time, however, community action was more vigorous, aided by institutional openings, by community activists and by a popular distaste for speculative office development. In this second period community action did score some successes. Ravetz (1980) describes the events surrounding the proposed redevelopment in Chesterfield, which consisted of demolishing listed buildings and an open-air market and replacing them with a shopping complex. These plans were shelved in 1974 after a petition had been signed by over 30,000 people and many thousands had attended a protest march. A similar success in another very 'visible' area with strong organised support was the Covent Garden story. In 1968 the GLC announced plans for the area which involved demolishing 60 per cent of the buildings and the construction of major new roadways, hotels, offices and a conference centre. In 1971 a public enquiry was held, at which there were over 128 objections led by the Covent Garden Community Association (CGCA) formed by residents, radical architects and planning students. The CGCA proposed alternative plans which emphasised conservation and housing. It also built up strong local ties, increasing local membership, opening a social centre, publishing a newsletter and establishing a community theatre. On the basis of community interests articulated by CGCA a revised plan was presented by the GLC in June 1976 but the CGCA criticised this plan and presented alternatives which attempted to maximise the degree of rehabilitation. Another revised plan was published later that year by the GLC and given approval by the CGCA, other local groups and finally by the GLC itself in June 1977. In this new plan the emphasis:

> . . . was one of sensitive renewal, emphasising rehabilitation and maximising housing, maintenance of the existing community, mixed uses and small scale. Office development was to be restrained and there were to be no new roads or hotels. . . . The plan was the diametric opposite of the 1968–1971 plan and a substantial scaling down of the June 1976 proposals. It can only be viewed as a triumph for the defenders of the community, a major reversal for property speculators and developers and a major concession by the planners and the GLC. (Christensen, 1981, p. 121)

Other stories abound. Wates (1976) tells the tale of Tolmers Square in the London Borough of Camden in which local residents groups in association with Labour party support managed to halt a major commercial redevelopment scheme. There were also failures. Ambrose and Colenutt (1975) describe the seemingly uninterrupted progress of 'the property machine' in both south London and Brighton, while in many cities office development has been scarcely affected by community action let alone successful community resistance. Lessons can be drawn from the successful examples. To be effective, as the Covent Garden example shows, community action has to be sustained and organised, while the case of Chesterfield shows that to be really successful large-scale political support has to be mobilised; Tolmer Square highlights the need for party political support.

Overall, the pace of urban renewal in contemporary urban Britain has decreased in recent years. Public housing policies pruned of investment now stress improvement rather than demolition and the private sector office boom has slumped. It would be a mistake however to see all this as a result of community pressure. The shifts from demolition to rehabilitation and from offices to conservation of the existing areas are as much due to changes in state policy, reduced levels of public spending and the recession as to community action.

The suburbanites

Much of the community action literature has focused on the inner city. There is good reason for this. Much action has taken place there and it has been of the kind which has given heart to radicals and activists. But this is only part of the story. The other major fault line in the city's geological structure is where city meets country. In the richer, owner-occupied, outlying districts community groups and amenity associations have been forming and acting. Here the main aim is to maintain exclusivity by keeping out new developments or changes to existing land use. A former chief planner of the Ministry of Housing and Local Government is said to have composed a mock grace for a Council of the Preservation of Rural England dinner (quoted in Cherry, 1982, p. 90). The grace went as follows:

> Lord, we thank thee in thy Grace
> For bringing us to this beauteous place;
> But one more thing, dear Lord, we pray,
> to keep all other folk away.

Such community concerns generally hinge around such slogans as 'no growth', 'not this type of growth', 'no growth here' and at an urban region level these groups are important in limiting the area for new housing or major public infrastructures.

Community action here consists of articulate groups mounting strong campaigns. It is here that community concerns are coupled most convincingly with property value considerations wrapped around the language of conservation and national interest. Gregory (1974) provides a useful case study of the deflection of the M4 motorway from the original proposal which took it over the Berkshire Downs north of Reading to the actual route which was constructed to the south of

Reading. This deflection was primarily due to the action of a strong, well-mounted campaign by local worthies. This type of pressure group activity is marked by its ability to turn issues into matters of national importance. In the case of the Third London Airport or the Vale of Belvoir enquiries, local community concerns were successfully transformed into issues of national importance.

Linking the two

The continued separations between residencies and work-places, play places and shopping centres have created much intra- and inter-urban movement. With the rise of the motor car as an important form of transport, the lobbying of the construction sector and the use of construction as a Keynesian regulator came the motorway solution to perceived transport problems. Throughout the late 1960s and early 1970s the construction of urban motorways was seen by planners as the principal means of improving mobility. An urban motorway was a technical solution by transport experts', a political choice favoured by central government and many local authorities eager to enhance their municipal image, and vigorously lobbied for by the construction industry. But motorways and motorway construction involve massive disruption to local communities. Although the community response, what Starkie (1982) calls the 'environmental backlash', could be seen as a subset of the types of community involvement already noted, it is of such importance both in the level of involvement and also in terms of its nature and consequences that it merits separate discussion.

In fact much community action in the late 1960s and early 1970s was a response to motorway proposals, and most of it from articulate, middle-income groups. In Winchester, for example, a ten-lane motorway was proposed in 1971 to run across the water meadows. An M3 Joint Action Group (JAG) was formed, mainly of middle-class, male, car-owning, long-established residents. Public demonstrations were mounted at a public enquiry and the whole need for the proposal was questioned. The M3 JAG mounted a sophisticated campaign, spending over £45,000 between 1973 and 1979 and hiring consultants to challenge the DOE figures. The motorway was never built. Anti-motorway campaigns also spilled over into formal political channels. In London in the late 1960s the GLC proposed a motorway solution to London's perceived transport problems. A public enquiry was held lasting over sixty-seven days at which local residents' groups presented evidence and the anti-motorway argument was presented by the London Motorway Action Group. In the 1970 GLC election, a Homes Before Roads party won 100,000 votes but no seats. However, the Homes Before Roads campaign continued and eventually forced both major political parties to come out against massive motorway construction.

The anti-motorway community response is interesting in a number of respects. Like others, where successful it was mainly led by middle-income articulate groups employing expert witnesses. Wealthy Winchester and fashionable London were the more obvious scenes of community success. But there were others. In unfashionable Carlisle a small local group with a mixed social base and few resources managed to save part of the city from being concreted over as a motorway (Gibson, 1979, p. 25–32).

Other areas were not so well organised nor so successful. But the strength of the anti-motorway protest led to major changes in official assessments. At the major public enquiries held throughout the early 1960s through to the mid 1970s protestors were not allowed to question the need for the motorway. But in the case of London and Winchester and other areas it was precisely the need for a motorway which was questioned, not just its likely consequences but its very *raison d'être*. An advisory committee on trunk road assessment was established in the wake of this anti-motorway dissent – the Leitch Committee (1977) – and in its report it suggested that objectors be allowed to question some of the bases of transport policy. Subsequent White Papers, while not meeting all the objections of the community groups, go some way to allowing community groups to question the need for a road scheme in a particular area. This signals a major change in policy which allows greater purchase for objections. If the motorway solution is ever proposed again on a similar scale the change in the rules will make for a more uncertain outcome.

The externality surface

The previous examples of community concern and action deal with the large, highly visible set pieces; the scenes of the city's 'tectonic activity'. But much community interest is within the 'plate' of residential areas concerned with small-scale, highly localised issues. We can picture the residential areas as an externality surface in which residencies are situated. The surface is composed of peaks where positive externalities are at their maximum and troughs where negative externalities predominate. The surface is constantly changing: a new sex shop here, greater traffic there all go to make up the changing land use surface which affect local residents. Many of the residents' reactions are attempts to manipulate this surface so that positive externalities are maximised and negative ones minimised. There is often potential conflict between areas as residents seek to halt a change, say the establishment of a bed-and-breakfast hostel for newly released prisoners, by suggesting it be moved elsewhere. The most effective monitors of the externality surface are the upper- and middle-income owner-occupiers with material interests at stake, who combine expertise and resources to form effective local lobbies. We can see an example of the consequences in the designation of conservation areas. These are areas in which demolition is strictly limited, new development must blend in with existing buildings and advertisements can be controlled. The conservation measures in effect are a series of negative controls but positive action is also forthcoming in the form of expenditure on housing and environmental improvement. By 1980 almost 4,600 conservation areas had been designated; half in villages and half in towns and cities. What seems to be happening is that the articulate middle-income residents of favoured commuter villages and fashionable inner suburbs have been successful in getting their neighbourhoods designated as conservation areas. In the villages the conservation measures have been used in conjunction with urban containment policies to protect the traditional character of the villages and to restrict further in-migration. In the cities the conservation area policies have been used by young, well-organised, local middle-class households in maintaining and improving their Victorian and Georgian neighbourhoods.

Declining public services – a new battle ground?

Much of the basis for the set piece community actions of the 1960s and 1970s has now disappeared. With the recession has come a self-imposed halt to the property machine and the motorway juggernaut. The case against motorways mounted by community groups, for example, is now more acceptable to politicians, as the costs of their provision spiral beyond the government's perceived ability to pay. The course of community action, British economic performance and government policy throughout the 1970s were in their different ways leading to the same destination. A more recent phenomenon, however, has been the decline in public services like education and nursery provision, hospitals and public transport, etc. Will this be the community battle ground of the 1980s? A number of factors would suggest a positive answer. The infrastructure of public participation and community action has been laid and as many people and groups rely upon public goods and services we may see some form of community resistence against the decline in public services. The degree of mobilisation will depend upon the issue, with the more visible, large-scale and sudden impacts such as hospital closure being more easy to contest than, say, gradual long drawn-out deterioration in medical care. However, there are a number of features which suggest the opposite. First, many of the more articulate groups able to use the formal political channels and public participation schemes may simply opt out of the public sector and move into the expanding private sectors for education and health provision. The rise of private health schemes and education although faced by problems of recession may take away a valuable part of the potential base of community action. Second, the language and practice of politics and industrial relations has lessened the need for a distinctive community response. To take just one example, cuts in social expenditure have provoked both public sector union action and Labour party condemnation. The politics of class may pre-empt the politics of place once again, and while community action may still occur much of the dialogue will doubtless take place through work-based and formal political channels. Third, the very existence of strong community groups may work against declining public services forming a terrain of struggle between the community and the authorities. In the 1960s to 1970s, as we have seen, the strategies of much community action were bound up with the provision of resources or with taking issue with public and private sector decisions. But in the 1980s a potential community response to declining public services is self-help, in which the community itself provides those services, such as the provision of nursery care, which the authorities are running down or closing. In this case community action is directed inwards, dealing with the consequences rather than combating the authorities directly. Thus, declining public services on their own may not provide the basis for a new round of community action although this does not rule out the emergence of community response in particularly sensitive areas where declining services may reach such a perceived level as to initiate a community response.

Non-action and failure

To focus on community action is of course to focus on the more visible signs of community concerns. It is just as important, however, to note that not all communities have reacted to urban renewal schemes, motorways, declining public services, etc. and not all have been successful. Non-action and failure are as much a feature of community politics in Britain as community action and success. Political exclusion is the fate of many lower-income households in Britain. Exclusion occurs because individual resentment is not crystallised in group action through lack of organisational skills, poor resources or simply resignation. Even when articulated, some demands are simply dismissed because they are not legitimated by the authorities. Given the obstacles and problems it is no wonder that only a few grievancies turn into articulated demands which are met by the authorities. Between the perception of a grievance and its resolution lie a large number of obstacles. The least successful groups in meeting these obstacles are the poor, the very badly-housed, the ill-educated and the unemployed, whose interests rarely appear high on the political agenda. The most successful groups are the rich and the wealthy who rarely need to organise since their interests are embedded into the dialogue and operation of public policy and private interest. Between these two extremes we can identify a range of community groups who have turned grievances into demands and have sought to transform demands into effects, the most successful being the well-organised who could speak the correct language, present the proper public image and exploit weakness in the opposition. The least successful were those fighting with a scanty organisation and few resources against strong and sustained opposition.

Community, capital and the state

In the previous section and previous chapters I have concentrated on examining capital, state and community in relative isolation. This was done for analytical purposes only, because in practice the interaction forms the seamless web of contemporary public life. In this final section I want to synthesise the three elements previously analysed. I will seek to show the broad outlines of the present sets of relationships and make some attempt at outlining possible future configurations. The exercise is tentative and provisional. The aim is not to identify future states but to pinpoint possible sets of unfolding relationships.

Capital and the state

The relationships between capital and the state are many and complex. Those which most directly involve community concerns centre on:

(1) Economic growth strategies.
(2) Land use planning.

These two have been shaped by the changing economic background and by shifts in political power at both national and local government levels.

(1) *Economic growth strategies.* In the 1960s and 1970s economic growth seemed assured: the problems were all to do with its rate and location. With a seemingly successful mixed economy, governments could afford to be sensitive to articulated demands from particular regions of the country. The degree of sensitivity varied from one political party to another and in general the Labour party was much more sensitive to these concerns, not least because much of its traditional support came from the poorer peripheral regions. Throughout the post-war period, and especially after 1960, regional policies were pursued in order to iron out the regional disparities in unemployment and wages caused by the poorer regions' declining industrial bases. These policies involved both sticks and carrots. Companies wishing to expand or move to new premises had to obtain industrial development certificates from central government and these were used to force expanding companies in the South-East and Midlands to move to the peripheral regions; they were supplemented by various grants, loans and subsidies, and together these measures shifted some manufacturing jobs to Scotland, Wales, Northern Ireland and the North of England. Over the period 1960–79 it has been estimated that between 250,000 and 350,000 jobs were created in these areas by regional policy measures. Measures were more rigorously pursued when the Labour party was in government. By the late 1970s regional policy was subject to severe criticism. From the Conservative Right spokesmen like Sir Keith Joseph could argue that £5,000 million had been pumped into regional subsidies but regional disparities still existed. The incoming Tory government in 1979 introduced a number of measures which reduced the regional policy programmes. The areas eligible for regional development grants were reduced. Figures 5.5 and 5.6 show the 'before' and 'after'

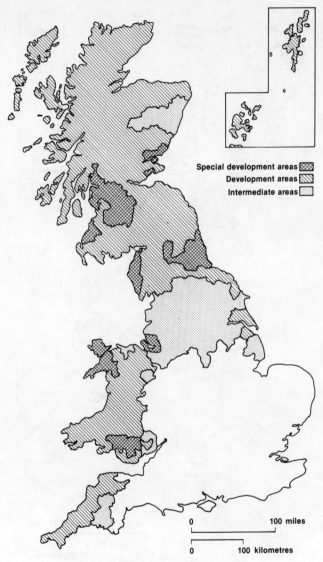

Special development areas
Development areas
Intermediate areas

0   100 miles

0   100 kilometres

FIGURE 5.5   *Assisted areas, pre-1982*

SOURCE: Department of Industry.

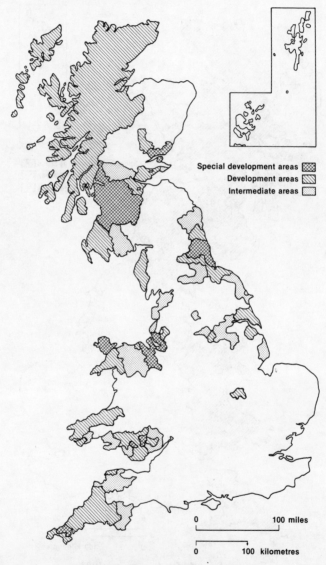

Special development areas
Development areas
Intermediate areas

0   100 miles

0   100 kilometres

FIGURE 5.6   *Assisted areas, post-1982*

SOURCE: Department of Industry.

picture. In 1977 the assisted areas covered 40 per cent of the
working population but only 25 per cent were included in the
new scheme. The regional development grant for new equipment and building was also reduced from 20 to 15 per cent and
the size of factory extensions for which firms needed an
industrial development certificate was increased five-fold.
Finally, 40 per cent was cut from the regional aid expenditure
programme, estimated to be £609 million by 1982–3. None of
these cuts provoked massive resistance partly because throughout the 1970s there had been mounting criticism of regional
policy from the political Left and from trade unions who
identified a number of flaws. In the first place there was little
public accountability in the way the grants were given and the
money was spent, and little room for discrimination. Some of
the world's biggest multinational companies were receiving aid
under this scheme. In the second place there was little
consideration given to the type of jobs created. Most of them
were low-paid, semi- and unskilled routine jobs, mostly using
female labour. In effect, multinational companies were using
the regional benefits to set up branch plants employing poorly
paid and poorly trained workers. Jobs were created but few of
them opened up opportunities for high-paid employment and
good training programmes. The jobs were tied into the branch
plant economy of multinationals, they were not laying the basis
for long-term self-sustaining economic growth in the depressed
regions.

The Conservative run-down of the regional programme was
not simply a matter of a response to its ineffectivity; there were
two further reasons, one general and one more specific.
Traditional regional policy is predicated upon the existence of
firms wishing to expand. The implementation of regional
policy thus involves the use of compulsion and persuasion to
move the growing firms in the South-East and the Midlands to
Scotland, Northern Ireland, etc. But as the recession has
widened and deepened, economic growth is no longer a
constant and firms wishing to expand are few and far between.
When growth falters governments tend to be more responsive
to the needs of capital and less sensitive to regional policy
arguments. Government seeks to nurture growth rather than
relocate it. The recession thus reduced the feasibility and

acceptability of traditional regional policy. More specifically, the Thatcher government was a government which drew its electoral support very largely from the more prosperous regions of the country, especially the well-to-do suburbs in the Home Counties. The swing to the Conservatives in the 1979 General Election was not a homogeneous one. North of the line from the Severn to the Wash the swing to the Conservatives was much weaker while in Scotland there was a slight swing to Labour. There was therefore very little electoral pressure on the Conservative government to pursue a vigorous regional policy which by definition aids Labour's heartland.

The regional pattern of economic growth and decline is a coarse-grained one. It masks differences at the subregional, especially the intra-urban, level. In the mid 1960s the concern of central government for uneven development was with its regional articulation, but by the mid 1970s the tension had focused on the inner city. The story of the inner city as a public policy area is an interesting one, showing both how economic decline has strengthened the demands of capital, while rising social unrest has forced a reconsideration. Here more clearly than for other areas, policies have been shaped according to the demands of accumulation and the need for legitimation.

The inner city programme is something of a misnomer. There has been no fully developed programme arising from a coherent intellectual and policy base, but rather a changing emphasis and commitment which has been perceived in varying ways at different times. This chameleon-like character needs to be borne in mind and the term 'programme' is used to define a constantly changing set of policy responses.

The inner city programme first got under way in 1968. The initial response was sparked by fears of racial unrest in inner city neighbourhoods. Urban America in the mid 1960s had provided a foretaste of what could happen in run-down neighbourhoods where poor blacks had poor housing and few opportunities. The first measure was the Urban Aid Programme announced in 1968. The aim was to provide money for education, housing, health and welfare in inner city areas of special social need. The initial impact was small and only £1.7 million had been spent on the 146 different schemes by 1974. The projects were small-scale, involving the provision of community welfare workers to help the people to help themselves. The inner city problem was perceived in terms of multiple deprivation and poor access to services and facilities. The response was to try to plug local people into the circuits of welfare Britain. A number of experiments were tried involving the Community Development Projects, Neighbourhoods Schemes, Quality of Life Projects and the Comprehensive Community Programme. These were experiments which seemed to provide solutions for the perceived problems without challenging vested interests or involving large amounts of public money. Throughout the 1970s this *mark I* inner city programme was proving to be inadequate. In the context of continued economic decline in the inner city the programme was merely cosmetic. Moreover, the reports of the Community Development Projects took on a much more radical flavour as they criticised the basic assumptions of the culture of poverty thesis and the notion of individual failure, social inadequacy and inefficient service provision as the roots of the problem. They pointed to the distribution of power within the society and the crucial importance of capital disinvestment from inner city areas. Against the background of rising unemployment and worsening conditions the Labour government began to recast the urban programme. The inner city programme *mark II* announced in 1977 was to involve more money in an attempt to renew the economic base of the inner city. The heart of this programme was to be special partnership schemes between central and local government in seven areas. In these areas the local authorities were to draw up spending plans concerned with capital-intensive projects providing the necessary physical infrastructure for attracting private capital back into the inner city. More than half the money was to be spent on laying out industrial estates and building advanced factory units. Here was the carrot of regional policy applied at the inner city level.

The urban programme *mark III* was introduced in 1980 by the Conservatives. The programme followed on from the mark II version by concentrating on subsidies to private capital but in a slightly revised form. First, new urban development corporations were set up in Merseyside and London docklands as the administrative means for spending public money to aid private capital. Second, the role of the state was transformed. Whereas previous governments had identified state response as a solution to the problems of the inner city the state was now seen as part of the problem. The new Conservative ideology represented planning controls and government regulations as strangleholds on economic growth. The answer was thus to minimise the role of government and introduce zones free from planning controls. In March 1980 the government announced that eleven enterprise zones were to be set up in areas of economic and physical decline (see figure 5.7). It was proposed

* Partnership schemes
□ Urban Development Corporations
△ The first enterprise zones*

FIGURE 5.7   *Urban policy impacts*

* For ones announced in 1982 see text.

that in these zones there would be 100 per cent capital allowance against tax for commercial and industrial buildings, exemptions from rates and requirements for industrial training, simplification of planning procedures, reduction in official requests for statistical information and exemption from development land tax. By reducing constraints it was hoped to free enterprise so that business would flourish, jobs be created and economic decline halted. A second batch of enterprise zones was announced in November 1982. These were in Allerdale (Cumbria), North-East Lancashire, Rotherham, Scunthorpe, Telford, North-East Derbyshire, Wellingborough (Northants), Middlesborough, and an area of North-West Kent including parts of Rochester, Gillingham and Gravesend.

The drift of Conservative inner city policy – and to an extent that of the previous Labour governments – was of an attempt to attract private capital back into the inner city. This involved expenditure on infrastructure and in effect was a direct subsidy from the state to capital. Overlying this was the Conservatives' attempt to reduce public expenditure and, as Figure 5.8 makes

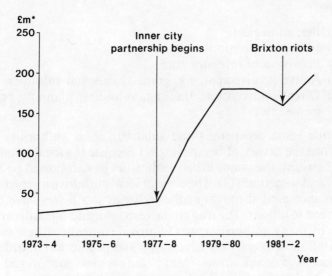

FIGURE 5.8 *Spending in the urban aid programme*

* 1979 prices.

clear, in the early years of the 1979 government the Urban Aid Programme was beginning to be run down. The riots in Bristol in 1980 and in Brixton in 1981 caused a reassessment of inner city policy. As Figure 5.8 also shows there was a marked increase in the amount spent on the Urban Aid Programme. This did not involve a complete reversal of the way money was spent. Concern was expressed, more money was put on the table, but this concern mediated through Conservative ideology resulted in yet more aid to private capital. While the demands of accumulation are to a certain extent being met the problems of legitimation in the inner city have been raised but not answered.

Any consideration of the relationship between state and capital needs to distinguish between the central and local levels of the state. While central government sets the overall context, local authorities have a potentially important role to play. The relationship between local government and capital has varied through time and across the country as local authorities differ in turning the potential into actual. Local authority relations to industrial promotion can be characterised by the following types:

(1) Benign neglect.
(2) Industrial promotion.
(3) Provision of infrastructure.
(4) Active involvement, e.g. grants, loans and subsidies.
(5) Direct intervention: training, subsidies, planning agreements, etc.

While some prosperous and suburban local authorities can afford the luxury of benign neglect because the local economy is buoyant, the major urban authorities have followed policies (2) and sometimes (3). The scale of local authority intervention has increased throughout the 1970s as job losses have continued to mount. The traditional response, and one still carried on by many authorities, was to provide more premises, and to spend more money on advertising and promotion in order to encourage small firms. Many authorities encouraged the establishment of small industrial parks and they were aided in this by the character of central government inner city policy. The partnership schemes were in a sense an attempt to forge a coherent relationship between central and selected local authorities in the promotion of policies (2) and (3) above. The problem for many authorities, however, is that as the recession has worsened the number of firms which can be attracted to selected sites is limited. One indication of this is the mounting level of publicity in the quality newspapers and financial press of an industrial promotion campaign as each local authority tries to sell its location and its workforce to a dwindling number of mobile firms (see Figure 5.9). Even then the firms may only stay as long as the grants and inducements continue. Take the example of Lee Jeans controlled by the VF corporation based in the United States. In 1970 the corporation opened a new plant in Greenock, Scotland. The local authority provided an attractive package: the company were exempt from any rents and rates for the first three years and only had to pay half rent and half rates for the next three years. The central government also provided grants to pay for 40 per cent of costs of new equipment and machinery, and the company was entitled to a government payment of £1.50 per week for each male and 75p a week for each female employee. The company was able to pay off its machinery bills with government-subsidised loans and to protect its export trade through the governments' export credit scheme. By the late 1970s, however, as the grants started to run out, the VF corporation attempted to shift its operations to Northern Ireland where more grants were obtainable. This leap-frogging by major multinational companies arises from the foot-loose nature of capital and the often desperate attempts of local authorities to attract new job-creating companies. Local authorities are in direct competition with each other, each trying to outbid the others in the level of incentives offered.

Some local authorities have reacted differently. A few Labour-controlled authorities, notably the London Wandsworth Borough between 1976 and 1978, and in the early 1980s the GLC, the West Midlands, South Yorkshire and Sheffield, have moved into implementing policies (4) and (5) cited above. These authorities have been given greater purchase on the local economy partly through the critique of traditional policies and partly by the scale of job loss and the inability of traditional policies to attract mobile firms to work.

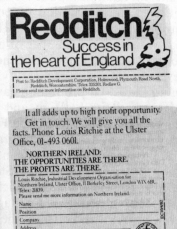

FIGURE 5.9   *Municipal promotion to attract capital*

SOURCE: Various advertisements in the Financial Press.

In the case of the Labour-controlled GLC, for example, an industry and employment committee was set up. It drew upon three main strands: the CDP work which highlighted the importance of large companies, the Left critique of traditional industrial policies as an aid to private capital and the articulated demands of the labour movement. The committee set up an enterprise board which invested in new forms of ownership like cooperatives, invested in specific sectors and signed planning agreements with major companies. Two examples can indicate the scale of its intervention (Ward, 1982). A furniture group threatened by the recession was going to go out of business with up to 400 redundancies. The GLC bought the factory for £1.25 million and gave a revenue support loan of £150,000 in return for two worker representatives on the board and negotiation of a planning agreement between the company, the TUC, the GLC and the new board. The factory reopened in 1982 with 120 jobs. The second example was an engineering plant threatened with closure by its parent company, GEC. The GLC funded a feasibility study on behalf of the workforce and gave a revenue support loan to enable the setting up of a workers' cooperative.

The net effect has been small. Only a few local authorities are adopting more radical strategies and the job creation schemes are only a drop in the rising ocean of unemployment. But they signify a substantial change in direction, involving more community and worker participation and the redefinition of the specific demands for job creation. Attention is now beginning to focus on the type of jobs, on the labour process itself and on alternative forms of ownership. These initiatives, although small in size and impact, are pregnant with political consequences. If more local authorities followed this course then there could be a swing in the balance of forces between capital and labour and between capital and the community.

(2) *Land use planning.* One of the main areas of state involvement in post-war Britain, compared to previous periods, is in its control over land development. Following a series of wartime reports, the first post-war Labour government introduced a series of Acts, the most important of which was the 1947 Town and Country Planning Act which nationalised

development rights. Henceforth those wishing to make a change of use to their land had to obtain planning permission. Permission was only given if it was in accord with the plan for the area drawn up by the local authorities. The drawing up of plans and the consequent use of development control (the name given to the system of granting or refusing planning permission) were the two main elements of the British land use planning system. Since its inception this system has been subject to various changes, deriving from the articulated interests of both capital and community as the planning system itself, with its control over land use development, became one of the main arenas of conflict.

The 1947 act gave plan-making and development control to the planning authorities of counties and county boroughs, who were asked to draw up twenty-year development plans indicating present and future patterns of land use. These plans were to be submitted to the central authorities for approval, in the early days to the Ministry of Housing and Local Government and later to the Department of the Environment (DOE). They were essentially blueprints guided by the ideas of the planning profession, chief among them being the need to separate out residential and non-residential land uses. Development control became a simple case of implementing the plans through granting or refusing planning permission where appropriate. When the planning system was constructed in the 1940s its architects envisaged only a minor role for the private sector. Development initiatives were to arise mainly from the actions of the public bodies. However, as the private sector, i.e. house builders in particular and the development industry in general, revived during the 1950s and expanded in the 1960s, more pressure was placed on the system. On the one hand there were more demands for the system to be responsive to the needs of developers. Much of the debate centred on the slowness of the planning system to provide decisions. But implicit in this discourse was the argument that the planning system should be tailored more closely to the needs of the private market. On the other hand there were demands for more participation from community groups and their national representatives who argued that planning was too 'top-down'. As then structured, the planning system gave little scope for public participation. The demands of the developers filtered through in the form of greater levels of land release in the 1960s, while the dual sets of demands of developers and community groups were expressed in the revised planning system introduced by the 1968 Town and Country Planning Act. This legislation obliged local authorities to draw up structure plans which were to be broad indications of major policy proposals and local plans for small areas detailing specific proposals. Structure plans were to be submitted to central government for approval. This new structure plan system opened the door to public debate. Being less precise than the old system, it gave developers greater room for disputing planning refusals while its statutory participation schemes enabled organised groups to voice their concern. Participation resulted not so much in a 'bottom-up' system but a 'middle-up' system, as the more articulate, better-organised groups used the public participation exercises to voice their opinion. In effect, land use planning changed from a blueprint system administered by professionals and ratified by politicians to a process of negotiation between private interests, sections of the community and the state.

The subsequent story is one of the rules of negotiation being changed by central government as it in turn is influenced by various pressure groups and as different political parties enter and leave office. The overall drift has been for central government to take a more permissive attitude in order to stimulate development. This has come about through two interrelated processes. One influential response to the recession has been to nurture and encourage the private sector. In planning terms this has involved reducing planning controls. The argument here is that the state through its planning controls has inhibited growth by imposing extra costs and delays on land development. This argument has of course been fostered by the developers themselves. The other process has been the emergence of strong organised lobbies, with the House Builders' Federation being particularly influential. These two processes fused into a single force after the election of the Conservative government in 1979. Senior politicians shared the goals of the developers and listened with ears attuned to developers' demands. The result in recent years has been a marked shift in the balance of forces towards building and property capital, which has been expressed in two main ways. First, the central government has itself modified structure plans. As we have already noted, structure plans are drawn up by local authorities and submitted to the DOE for approval and ratification by the Secretary of State: and he has intervened to change recent structure plan submissions. Take the case of central Berkshire, where the structure plan was started in 1974 and submitted in 1978. As the legislation required, there was a public participation exercise in so far as the preferred strategies were advertised, exhibited and discussed in the local media and through a series of public meetings. In the structure plan three strategies were outlined:

(1) *Limited growth*, leading to a population in the mid 1980s of between 420,650 and 436,500.
(2) *Restricted growth* with a target population by the mid 1980s of between 399,600 and 416,200.
(3) *High growth*, with population reaching between 471,900 and 491,900 in the 1980s.

Notice that a no growth option was not offered: and yet the majority of individuals and organisations involved in the public participation scheme was against uncontrolled growth. Of the fifty-three organisations who voiced an opinion 50 per cent called for limited growth, 19 per cent for restricted growth and 31 per cent for a mixture of limited and restricted growth strategies. The strategy adopted by the county council was the limited growth strategy, involving 32,000 extra dwellings. This structure plan was submitted to the DOE in June 1978 and approval was given in April 1980. But a number of modifications had been made. Most important was the requirement made by the Secretary of State that the county council identify land for an extra 8,000 houses on major sites over and above the initial figure of 32,000 dwellings for development. This arose from the objections and demands raised by builders. An extra 8,000 dwellings meant an extra population of 20,000, the equivalent to a small-sized town. The local press quickly dubbed it 'Heseltown' after the then Secretary of State at the DOE, Michael Heseltine. Although the local authority was against the change it could do little. The DOE had the power to enforce central government wishes through the development control system. Most changes of land use require planning permission which is given by the local authority, but if rejected an applicant can then appeal to the DOE who can overturn local authority planning decisions. Given this ultimate sanction, the local authority in central Berkshire had little option but to accept the extra 8,000 houses. If it had not, it would have been faced with developers putting in planning applications which, when rejected by the local planning committee, would have been repealed by the DOE. Far better, the council argued, to identify sites suitable for development and consistent with overall planning objectives than suffer development on appeal. The case of central Berkshire is not an isolated example. Many local authorities currently submitting structure plans are having modifications which, while not of a similar magnitude, are in the same overall direction. The example highlights the essential power of central government. In effect the modification of the structure plan involved the imposition of central control over local representation, and as such lends further support to Saunders's hypothesis (see p. 66).

Second, there have been more pervasive attempts at changing the balance. In public pronouncements ministers have sought to effect a change in the overall climate of planning. In addressing the Royal Town Planning Institute in 1979, for example, the Tory minister at the DOE, Michael Heseltine, noted:

> the apparatus of planning control seems to have grown bigger and more complicated . . . This country, in economic terms, cannot afford the manpower involved in a system which in some parts can be negative and unresponsive But above all, we cannot afford the economic process of delayed investment, whether commercial, domestic or industrial.

The new attitude has also been outlined in government circulars. These are written statements sent by the DOE to local authorities giving advice on planning and related matters. While technically the circular is only of an advisory nature, it is nevertheless a potent device. Failure at the local level to implement circular advice may lead to appeals which are then decided by the DOE. Such appeals can be costly and can encourage haphazard decisions and it is thus in the interests of the local authority to comply with these circulars. It is through the medium of the circular in particular that we can detect a gradual shift in land use planning towards a more explicit incorporation of developers' interests in the very structure of land use planning procedures. In 1970 a DOE circular (10/70) requested that local planning and housing authorities should release more land for private house building. A 1972 circular asked local authorities to release yet more land and in 1978 local authorities were asked to see that regular meetings were held as often as possible with builders. An acceleration in this tendency has been signalled by the circulars distributed in 1980. Circular 9/80 requested local authorities to work jointly with developers to agree a schedule of sites which would provide a five-year supply of housing land. Circular 22/80 stated that the availability of five-year supply was not necessarily sufficient reason for refusing planning permission on other sites. This latter circular placed more emphasis on the possibilities of allowing higher densities and in general asked local authorities to take a more positive attitude to planning applications. As the circular noted,

> The Government want to make sure that the planning system is as positive and helpful as it can be to investment and industry and commerce and to the development industry. Development should be prevented or restricted only where this serves a clear planning purpose and the economic effects have been taken into account. (DOE, 1980)

These recent circulars are all concerned to speed up the planning decision process and make the whole system more responsive and sensitive to developers' interests.

While the overall trend has been for the role and practice of planning to be shifted towards the needs of developers, this has not been a simple straight-line progression. The voice of community concern has been heard at both national and local levels. At national level, for example, there have been successive attempts to obtain public benefit from the private profits made through the planning system. Since the very action of land use planning in a market economy allows profits to be made – once landowners have been given planning permission they can sell at a much higher price than would be the case if this permission had not been granted – the operation of the planning system has come under close scrutiny. In the original 1947 Act, for example, a betterment levy of 100 per cent on the gain in value before development took place was charged by a central land board. When they came to power in 1951, the Conservatives dismantled the existing system; the betterment levy was dropped in 1953 and the role of the central land board was restricted to that of compensation. From 1959 the compensation paid to landowners was to be calculated on the basis of full market value rather than as previously on existing use value. By these acts the Conservatives reduced public gain from the planning system and allowed greater private profits to be made from development. A second attempt to tax private gains was made by the Labour government in the mid 1960s. Under the 1967 Land Commission Act a betterment levy of 40 per cent was charged on development gains and a new body, the Land Commission, was given powers to acquire a 'land bank' which was to be used to release land for development. The scheme proved to be a failure. Relations between local authorities and the Land Commission were tense and not enough money was given to the Commission, while landowners withheld land hoping for a change of government. In 1971 the Tories scrapped the Commission and repealed the betterment levy. With few controls and a property boom in the early 1970s, the way was clear for vast speculative gains to be made out of land dealing and land development. This experience strengthened the argument of those in the Labour party arguing for more control of private gains via the planning system. In a White Paper on land the incoming Labour government of 1974 committed itself to tax the windfall profits of redevelopment gains and control more closely the whole process of land development. Between the promise and the reality, however, fell the shadow of pressure group activity. The powerful property lobby worked against the schemes and the resulting legislation, the Community Land Act, was weak in relation to the initial promise. Under the Act, local authorities were required to purchase land which had been given planning permission at current market values. The authority could then decide when to develop the land and who should be involved. Under this scheme it was hoped that windfall gains from planning decisions would find their way into the coffers of the local authority rather than the hands of property dealers. The reality was different. The scheme was hamstrung from the beginning by lack of resources and by the need to make a profit on the land dealings. The initial level of funding was small and was further reduced in December 1976 when expenditure was reduced from £76.7 million in 1976–7 to £38 million for 1977–8. The scheme was increasingly seen as marginal to government concerns and the political uncertainty regarding its future did little to aid full implementation. Any assessment of the performance of the community land scheme would have to pronounce it a failure. One of the first things the Conservatives did on coming to power in 1979 was scrap the Community Land Act and initiate a change in emphasis in land use planning towards developers.

At the local level, planning authorities have sought to use their power in obtaining benefits. Many authorities have only granted planning permission to developers if some measure of planning gain is introduced: for example, a company applying to build an office block may be given planning permission only if it also builds twenty old people's homes or provides a playground or pays for access roads. Throughout the 1970s, this relationship between developers and planning authorities became a common practice in some areas. Planning gains have became so routinised that developers often introduce planning gain measures into their applications. In this way planning authorities lever benefits from developers; the greater the developers' need and the stronger the authorities resolve, the greater the leverage. The whole issue of planning gain has been recently changed, however, by the attitude of the central government. Developers refused planning permission through their failure to provide enough planning gain may be assured of a warm response through the planning appeals procedure. The overall change in climate has strengthened developers' hands and weakened those of authorities seeking to lever planning gain.

The practice and procedure of land use planning is thus a system of negotiation, an arena for competing social interests. The planning system is an important seismograph of changing social forces. Throughout the post-war period we have seen a gradual and emerging tendency for planning to change in order to accommodate both developers' interests and community concerns. Changes in the nature of accommodation have been mainly the result of changes in national political power.

Community and capital

Communities rarely take on capital interests in single combat. The conflicts and tensions between capital and community are played out within the arena of the state. Both negotiate the state apparatus and seek to influence political decision-makers. In most cases the contest is unequal. Companies, property interests, etc. have more resources, better access to formal channels of decision-making and their values are embedded in the dominant world view in so far as the rights of property and the needs of capital are implicitly and explicitly accepted by most people. While community groups may have to protest and lobby, capital interests rarely have to since their aims are served by the normal working of the market and the state. The conflict is also unequal in the sense that community groups rarely have the power to exact much out of capital directly. The power of communities is reactive and limited to lobbying resource-holders and political decision-makers. Capital, in contrast, can both lobby and offer tangible benefits in the form of new jobs, new buildings, larger rate payments, etc. While capital can present the face of a benefactor, then, community groups are often seen by the political élite and the media as troublesome, greedy activists.

But capital needs the state. Builders and property developers, for example, need planning permission and it is at this juncture, this part in the complex interaction, that community groups can influence events. By lobbying councillors and MPs and by making protests they can strengthen the hand of the state in its dealings with capital. This has been manifest not only in the more dramatic events such as Covent Garden but in the changing nature of, say, land use planning. Throughout the 1970s planning gain was as much a feature of community action as the set piece battles.

Community groups have been hampered in their fights with capital by their failure to form alliances with the labour movement. A community activist in London describes a common situation:

> Throughout the eight years in Notting Hill efforts were made by the People's Association group to ask for support for community struggles from local workers, and to give support to local workers in strike situations. . . . However, the integration of these struggles was never given much time or energy and was not even seen as an integral part of the struggle by either the local groups or the local trade unionists. (O'Malley, 1977, p. 179)

The difficulties in forging links between the labour movement and community groups are many. Even where interests coincide – and there are many instances where they do not – there are severe organisational problems in linking routinised male-dominated, hierarchically-ordered, production-orientated systems of representation with ephemeral, small-scale, localised, often more democratic movements. Behind the split there also lie gender differences. The labour movement is still dominated by men and its failure to link up with community groups is partly a reflection of the sexual division of labour and partly a sexist inability to consider problems centring on the home and the residential area. However, recent years have seen new alliances being fused in certain cities, especially where the pressures of commercial land development and the rate and scale of job loss provide a common platform for union and community activists. In much of urban Britain the localised effects of the recession and restructuring in conjunction with urban renewal and declining public services are providing the potential basis for links to be drawn between home-based and work-based struggles. In some cases the link has already effectively been made (see Craig *et al.*, 1979).

Community and the state

Community concerns are local concerns. Concern is turned into action through a number of factors but for action to be successful communities and their representatives must win over decision-makers and resource-providers. In most cases the key figures are in the local authority. The purchase which community groups can achieve on the local political machine depends upon:

(1) The nature of the community group and its strategies.
(2) The receptivity of councillors and majority council opinion to community demands.

We can imagine a continuum of councillor reaction from active involvement and encouragement through indifference to explicit hostility. More radical councillors will help tenants' organisations and local cooperatives who would be politically excluded by the more reactionary Conservative and Labour councillors. In similar vein, Conservative councils are more likely to encourage and reflect ratepayers' groups and exclusionary community groups. At the local political level community groups are used in turn to legitimate local council action. There is a two-way traffic between community organisations and local political representation. There are frequently important ties, often formed by the same individuals in different capacities, between community organisations and local political parties.

The relative success of groups depends upon how far they can influence the local system. And this is a function of their strength and degree of legitimation afforded to them by the local politicians. The different strategies adopted by community groups, which can range from collaborative to coercive, depend in turn upon the response from the local council. Many groups start out with collaborative strategies, more successful ones carry on with them as they seem to be working while the less successful groups may be forced into more coercive strategies. This may prove to be either a route to success if the issue is made more visible and captures the public imagination or it may lead to the stigmatisation of the group by 'responsible' councillors. It is a difficult decision for many groups. In this line of argument the least successful groups would be the most vociferous, forced by the inaction of the authorities to further action and civil disobedience. This does not necessarily follow. Those unable to achieve any purchase, like the Beckton protest described by Dunleavy (1977), are forced through a recognition of their lack of power into inaction. If local authorities are completely unresponsive then community groups on their own are unlikely to achieve anything. Lack of explicit community action may be a sign of failure. It may also be a symbol of success as the more affluent communities may not need to be involved in community action. In this case the lack of action reflects a community whose interests are already well served.

In the past there was a general if not perfect fusion of interests between neighbourhoods and political representation. The local Conservative party broadly reflected the upper- and middle-income suburban areas while the majority Labour representation gave voice to the demands of inner city dwellers. In recent years all this has changed as cities have expanded, council estates have grown up in the periphery, gentrified areas are emerging in the inner city and overall, residential differentiation is continuing apace. The broad mesh of political representation has failed to capture in its entirety the very localised concerns of all these different areas. Thus Conservative councils were a target of middle- and upper-income community groups affected by motorway plans while inner-city residents were often fighting Labour councils in their battle against urban renewal. The rise of community groups and community action has arisen because of the failure of local interests to be adequately represented in the political system which in turn reflects the broad nature of political representation in Britain as set against the growing size and complexity of neighbourhood concerns.

Community groups are not only involved with the local authorities. We can make a further elaboration between central and local government and community groups. A range of relationships is described in Table 5.3. For the sake of simplicity a single community and a unitary central and local government are posited, although in practice there are many communities and distinctions can be drawn between officers

TABLE 5.3   *Community and the state: ideal relationships*

	1	2	3	4	5
Local state	—	X	X	O	X
Central state	X	X	—	X	O
Community	O	O	O	O	O

O: For community;   X: against community;   —: indifferent.

and members and between the different government departments. From this simple, idealised model, however, five types
of relationships can be identified. In the case of (1) communities are in conflict with central government with local
authorities being indifferent or unable to interfere. Such cases
are rare since community concerns generally have some local
political impact if the matter comes to the attention of the
central government. More common is the case of (3) where
central government is indifferent to a conflict between local
government and a community group. In the case of (2)
community is up against central and local government as in the
heyday of urban renewal schemes. However, in the case of (4)
and (5) the central and local government line up differently as
regards the concerns of the community. These cases are
becoming more common. Previously, there were isolated
examples but these are now becoming more frequent as the
major political parties move away from the middle ground of
the post-war consensus. Differences between local and central
government in political pursuasion thus become more important and more fundamental. Community concerns can overlie
and reinforce the splits between central and local government.
In the case of (4) we can imagine a Left-wing local authority
backing community demands for cheaper public housing,
lower fares on public transport and more welfare-type expenditure against a Conservative central government. Conversely, a
Conservative central government may lend support, say
through the development control appeals procedure, to suburban community groups fighting against public housing
estates proposed by a Labour local authority. Community
concerns are now not only against the 'state': they involve

different levels of the state often in opposition one to another.

In terms of political consequences two very broad types of community action can be identified. First, there are those which are non-disruptive of existing social and political relations. The community organisations of the rich and wealthy which maintain local exclusivity, for example, buttress and reinforce the distribution of real income, power and life chances in society. Much successful community action has been of this type. Second, there are those forms of community organisation and action which question the existing relations. The definition of such radical groups is that if successful they involve a redistribution of power, real income and life chances. Much of the community literature has focused almost entirely on this latter category. Two general positions can be outlined. There are those who stress the limitations of such community action. They argue that community concerns are isolated from the labour movement, have limited objectives, are small and weak while being issue- and locality-specific. All this is true and on their own radical community groups are unlikely to achieve a large redistribution of power. But this is to ignore the scope and potential of radical community action. The second perspective, and one which I hold, is to look beyond the naïve belief that the labour movement *as presently structured and on its own* can effect a major and real transformation of power. A strongly hierarchical, male-dominated, production-orientated system of representation can effect changes in the capital— labour relation inside the factory gates and if successful it could bring a top-down form of industrial democracy. But it is less sensitive to community concerns which are local and which effect everyone and particularly non-waged women, children, adolescents, old people. Radical community action has not only involved non-wage groups but has been relatively success-ful in introducing real democratic discussion and participation in organisations. Radical community action has proved to be an important consciousness-raising exercise giving people an experience of how to question existing arrangements and pose alternatives. The wider potential of community action is that as a subjective experience it involves a transformation of attitude and alternative forms of organisation while incorpor those ignored by the labour movement. If socialists really 'power to the people' then the experience of radical community action, albeit on the small scale at which it has so far occurred, should be fostered and encouraged. The socialists of the 1980s should be looking to fuse the power of the organised labour movement, the mass political representation of the Labour party, with radical community groups, the women's movement and oppressed ethnic minorities. There is life as well as a radical tradition and experience outside the factory gates and the council chambers. The task in fusing these diverse groups, in going 'beyond the fragments' is enormous and the difficulties many. But the prize is high.

Guide to Further Reading

The context (Chapter 2)

The economic conditions of the end of the post-war boom are given an international coverage by Mandel (1978). The general background to economic decline in Britain is well covered by Aaronowitch *et al.* (1981) and Gamble (1981). Considerations on Britain's post-war economic performance include Caves and Krause (1980) and Beckerman (1979). More detailed studies are available in Blackaby (1979), Glyn and Sutcliffe (1972), Glyn and Harrison (1980), Eatwell (1982) and Bacon and Eltis (1976).

The standard work on the management of the British economy is Blackaby (1978); but see also Brittan (1964) and Stewart (1978). Pollard (1982) makes the strongest case for the sacrifice of industry to 'the city'.

Regular assessments of economic performance appear in *The Economist* (weekly), *National Institute Economic Review* (quarterly), the *Cambridge Economic Policy Review* (annually) and the *Bank of England Quarterly Bulletin*. Official statistics are available in *Financial Statistics, Economic Trends, Economic Progress Report* (monthly); see also the *Monthly Digest of Statistics* and the *Annual Abstract of Statistics* published by the Central Statistical Office.

The politics of economic decline are discussed in Alt (1979) and Dahrendorf (1981). The facts of post-war politics are available in Butler and Sloman (1980). The rise of the new Right is well covered in Gamble (1981), placed in sociological context by Hall (1979), while its intellectual basis can be uncovered in Hayek (1982), Friedman (1977) and the series of papers published by the Institute of Economic Affairs (IEA). See Hall and Jacques (1983) for a series of informative papers on the politics of Thatcherism.

Labour's alternative economic strategy is discussed in various publications: see Benn (1979), Blake and Ormerod (1980), Cripps *et al.* (1981), Labour party (1981) and CSE (1980).

The founding members of the SDP have all written books on their philosophy; see Rodgers (1982) and Owen (1981). A critical survey of the SDP and its relationship with the intellectual socialist heritage is given by Samuel (1982).

180

On the mood of Britain in an era of no growth, public expenditure reduction and high unemployment see Crick (1981) and Jordan (1982).

The response of capital (Chapter 3)

The best general introduction to capital in Britain is Aaronovitch *et al.* (1981). On specific aspects: see Aaronovitch and Sawyer (1975), Hannah (1976) and Hannah and Kay (1977), on growing concentration; Morgan (1979) on the international dimension of British companies; and Holland (1975) on the new meso-economic power. Reasons for the poor investment performance are discussed by Glyn and Sutcliffe (1972). The extent and effects of British overseas investment are noted in Dunning (1979).

The literature on the effects of restructuring is immense and growing. Blackaby (1979) has edited a general set of papers while Friend and Metcalf (1981) adopt a radical posture and Fothergill and Gudgin (1982) present the empirical results of the spatial reordering of the economy. The militant response of labour is chronicled by Coates (1981). Massey and Meegan (1982) examine the reasons for and implications of job loss. More detailed work includes case studies of sectors, see Massey and Meegan (1979) for a case study of the electrical engineering sector and Friedman (1977) on the car industry. Examples of work on particular places include studies of older industrial areas (CDP, 1977b), and inner city areas (Dennis 1978; Keeble, 1978); work on particular cities includes Liverpool (Merseyside Socialist Research Group, 1980), North Shields (North Tyneside CDP, 1978) and Lancaster (Murgatroyd, 1981). See Martin (1982) for a discussion of the regional pattern of job loss. A handy source of information is the local authority structure plans with subsequent reviews which provide data on the state of the local economies.

A short readable account of industrial relations in Britain is given by Crouch (1979). The arguments for more privatisation are present in an IEA (1979) publication.

The rise of the big financial institutions is discussed in Plender (1982). Bain (1981) looks at the city from a conventional stance while one of the best sources of information on the functioning of the institutions is the Wilson Report (1980). The changing pattern of investment opportunity is recorded in the weekly *Investors' Chronicle*.

The state (Chapter 4)

Jessop (1980) and Sampson (1982) provide two contrasting introductions to the state in post-war Britain. *The Economist* (1980) brief on political Britain contains useful information.

The politics of economic decline

Alt (1979) discusses the findings of public opinion polls while the changing economic policies are discussed in Stewart (1978), and Dahrendorf (1981) makes some general comments. The effects of economic decline are discussed in a brief but readable paper by King (1982) while a longer analysis of the general political realignment is Sarlvik and Crewe (1983). The effects on the individual political parties include Kavanagh (1982) on Labour and Behrens (1980) on the Conservative party. Bradley (1981) and Stephenson (1982) discuss the rise of the SDP.

Getting and spending

The introductions to the British taxation system which are aware of its redistributional consequences include Field *et al.* (1977) and Pond (1982).

The literature on public expenditure is now vast: an inside seat is given by a former Treasury official, Pliatzky (1982a); Heclo and Wildavsky (1981) provide an invaluable guide to intra-governmental wheeling and dealing; Bennett (1982) looks at the spatial RSG variation in public finance; Gough (1979) is one of the best guides to the economics of the modern welfare state in Britain; and for a sample of works on the politics and economics of public spending and public expenditure cutbacks see CSE (1979), CIS CDP (1975), Hood and Wright (1981), Walker (1982) and Wright (1980). Basic information is available in the government spending plans published annually and most of the empirical material in this chapter was taken from Treasury (1982).

The fiscal relationships between central and local government are discussed in Greenwood (1981), Midwinter and Page (1981), Burgess and Travers (1980) and Newton (1981). Kaufman (1982) provides an opposition back-bench viewpoint. More general treatments of local governments and their relationship with the central authorities include Bennington (1976), Dearlove (1979), Dunleavy (1980), Elliot (1981), Saunders (1980, 1981, ch. 8) and Short (1982a, chs 5 and 6).

For the general background to the growth of the public sector unions see Crouch (1979) and Taylor (1980). Pliatzky (1982b) discusses cash limits while Eltis (1982) reassesses the Bacon–Eltis thesis.

Reproducing the social order

For general introductions to education see Kogan (1978) and Byrne *et al.* (1975).

The best introduction to the role and practice of the British judiciary is Griffith (1981). On the law and order theme see Hall *et al.* (1978) and Thompson (1980). A sympathetic account of the police is given by Reiner (1978) while more critical studies include Bunyan (1981). The riots are examined by the Scarman Report (1981), Rex (1982) and Cowell *et al.* (1982) and in special issues of *Political Quarterly* (vol. 53 nos, 1982) and *Race and Class* (vol. XXIII, nos 2 and 3, 1981).

The mass media is producing a burgeoning literature; see Gureivitch *et al.* (1982), Tulloch (1982) and Whale (1977). Examinations of the news include Philo *et al.* (1982) and Hartley (1982). On the local press see Murphy (1976) and Cox and Morgan (1974).

Community concerns (Chapter 5)

The rise of community action

The theme of environment is a large one. For discussions which tie in with the exposition of this chapter see O'Riordan (1980), Johnson (1973), Kimber and Richardson (1974) and Sandbach (1980).

Theoretical discussions of the rise and importance of community action include Castells (1978), Cowley *et al.* (1977), Saunders (1979) and Katznelson (1981). General observations on community action in Britain are available in Barker (1979), Butcher *et al.* (1980), Gibson (1979) and Hain (1976). See also the journal *Community Action* and the regular Community Work Series published by Routledge & Kegan Paul in association with the Association of Community Workers: among the more important issues are Craig *et al.* (1979, 1982), Curno (1978) and Smith and Jones (1981).

Community action in the city

Dunleavy (1981) provides the most comprehensive account of
council housing redevelopment schemes. There is a welter of case
studies on property development and community action: for useful
case studies see Ambrose and Colenutt (1975) and Christensen
(1979); Kirby (1982) provides a general introduction to the politics of
externalities and Hall (1982) to planning decisions. More specific
examples include Starkie (1982) on motorways and Short (1982b) on
housing.

Community, capital and the state

Much of the material in this section is taken from Short (1982c).

Regional policies are covered by Keeble (1976) and Frost and
Spence (1981) while Lawless (1981) provides a comprehensive
account of inner city policies.

Enterprise zones are discussed by various authors; see
International Journal of Urban and Regional Research (vol. 6, no. 3,
1982). On the economic initiatives of the Left local authorities see, for
example, Craig *et al.*, 1979) and for general discussion of the local
state and the local economy see Massey (1982) and CDP (1979).

The most useful introduction to recent changes in the land use
planning system is the discussion paper published by the Council for
the Protection of Rural England (CPRE, 1981).

On moving beyond the fragments see Rowbotham *et al.* (1979).

Bibliography

Aaronovitch, S. and Sawyer, M. (1975) *Big Business: Theoretical and Empirical Aspects of Concentration and Mergers in the United Kingdom* (London: Macmillan).

Aaronovitch, S. and Smith, R. with J. Gardiner and R. Moore (1981) *The Political Economy of British Capitalism* (London: McGraw-Hill).

Abercrombie, N., Hill, S. and Turner, B. S. (1980) *The Dominant Ideology Thesis* (London: Allen & Unwin).

Alderman, G. (1978) *British Elections* (London: Batsford).

Alt, J. E. (1979) *The Politics of Economic Decline: Economic Management and Political Behaviour in Britain since 1964* (Cambridge: Cambridge University Press).

Ambrose, P. and Colenutt, B. (1975) *The Property Machine* (Harmondsworth: Penguin).

Arnstein, S. R. (1971) 'A Ladder of Citizen Participation in the USA', *Journal of the Town Planning Institute*, vol. 57, pp. 176–82.

Bacon, R. and Eltis, W. (1976; 2nd edn 1978) *Britain's Economic Problem: Too Few Producers* (London: Macmillan).

Bain, A. D. (1981) *The Economics of The Financial System* (London: Martin Robertson).

Barker, A. (1976) *The Local Amenity Movement* (London: Civic Trust).

Barker, A. (1979) *Public Participation in Britain* (London: Bedford Square Press).

Beckerman, W. (ed.) (1979) *Slow Growth in Britain* (Oxford: Clarendon Press).

Behrens, R. (1980) *The Conservative Party From Heath to Thatcher* (London: Saxon House).

Benn, A. (1979) *Arguments for Socialism* (London: Jonathan Cape).

Bennett, R. (1982) *Central Grants to Local Governments* (Cambridge: Cambridge University Press).

Bennington, J. (1976) *Local Government Becomes Big Business* (London: CDP).

Blackaby, F. T. (ed.) (1978) *British Economic Policy 1960–74* (Cambridge: Cambridge University Press).

Blackaby, F. T. (ed.) (1979) *Deindustrialisation* (London: Heinemann).

Blake, P. and Ormerod, J. (1980) *The Economics of Prosperity* (London: Grant McIntyre).

Bradley, I. (1981) *Breaking the Mould? The Birth and Prospects of the Social Democratic Party* (Oxford: Martin Robertson).

Brittan, S. (1964) *The Treasury Under The Tories 1951–1964* (Harmondsworth: Penguin).

Buckley, P. J. and Pearce, R. D. (1977) 'Overseas Production and Exporting by the World's Largest Enterprises—A Study in Sourcing Policy', Discussion Paper, Department of Economics, University of Reading.

Bunyan, T. (1981) 'The Police Against the People', *Race and Class*, vol. XXIII, pp. 153–70.

Burgess, T. and Travers, T. (1980) *Ten Billion Pounds: Whitehall's Takeover of the Town Halls* (London: Grant McIntyre).

Butcher, M., Collis, P., Glen, A. and Sills, P. (1980) *Community Groups in Action* (London: Routledge & Kegan Paul).

Butler, D. E. and Sloman, A. (1980) *British Political Facts* (London: Macmillan).

Byrne, D., Williamson, W. and Fletcher, B. (1975) *The Poverty of Education* (Oxford: Martin Robertson).

Castells, M. (1978) *City, Class and Power* (London: Macmillan).

Caves, R. E. and Krause, L. B. (eds) (1980) *Britain's Economic Performance* (Washington D.C.: Brookings Institution).

Cherry, G. (1982) *The Politics of Town Planning* (London: Longman).

Christensen, T. (1979) *Neighbourhood Survival: The Struggle for Covent Garden's Future* (London: Prism Press).

Christensen, T. (1981) 'The Politics of Redevelopment: Covent Garden', in D. T. Herbert and R. J. Johnston (eds), *Geography and The Urban Environment*, vol. 4 (London: Wiley).

CIS CDP Special Report (1975) *Cutting The Welfare State: Who Profits?* (London: Counter Information Services and Community Development Project Information and Intelligence Unit).

Coates, K. (1981) *Work-ins, Sit-ins and Industrial Democracy* (Nottingham: Spokesman).

Cockburn, C. (1977) *The Local State* (London: Pluto Press).

Community Development Project (CDP) (1977a) *Gilding The Ghetto* (London).

Community Development Project (CDP) (1977b) *The Costs of Industrial Change* (London).

Community Development Project (CDP) Political Economy

Collective (1979) *The State and The Local Economy* (Nottingham: Russell Press).

Conference of Socialist Economists (CSE) London Working Group (1980) *The Alternative Economic Strategy* (London: CSE Books and Labour Co-ordinating Committee).

Conference of Socialist Economists (CSE) State Group (1979) *Struggle Over The State: Cuts and Restructuring in Contemporary Britain* (London: CSE Books).

Council for the Protection of Rural England (CPRE) (1981) 'Planning—Friend or Foe?', CPRE Countryside Discussion Paper.

Cowell, D., Jones, T. and Young, J. (1982) *Policing The Riots* (London: Junction).

Cowley, J., Kaye, A., Mayo, M. and Thompson, M. (1977) *Community or Class Struggle* (London: Stage 1).

Cox, H. and Morgan, D. (1974) *City Politics and the Press* (Cambridge: Cambridge University Press).

Craig, G., Derricourt, N. and Loney, M. (eds) (1982) *Community Work and The State* (London: Routledge & Kegan Paul).

Craig, C., Mayo, M. and Sharman, N. (eds) (1979) *Jobs and Community Action* (London: Routledge & Kegan Paul).

Crick, B. (ed.) (1981) *Unemployment* (London: Methuen).

Cripps, F., Griffith, J., Morrell, F., Reid, J., Townsend, P. and Weir, S. (1981) *Manifesto: A Radical Strategy For Change* (London: Pan).

Crouch, C. (1979) *The Politics of Industrial Relations* (London: Fontana).

Curno, P. (ed.) (1978) *Political Issues and Community Work* (London: Routledge & Kegan Paul).

Dahrendorf, R. (1981) 'The Politics of Economic Decline', *Political Studies*, vol. XXIX, pp. 284–91.

Davies, J. G. (1975) 'Whose Grass Roots? Citizens, Councillors and Researchers', in P. Leonard (ed.), *The Sociology of Community Action*, Sociological Review Monograph 21, University of Keele.

Dean, M. (1982) 'Making the Link Between Crime and Unemployment', *Guardian*, 1 August, p. 17.

Dearlove, J. (1979) *The Reorganisation of Local Government* (Cambridge: Cambridge University Press).

Dennis, R. (1978) 'The Decline of Manufacturing Employment in Greater London 1966–74', *Urban Studies*, vol. 15, pp. 63–73.

Department of the Environment (DOE) (1980) *Development Control—Policy and Practice*, DOE circular 22/80.

Dunleavy, P. (1977) 'Protest and Quiescence in Urban Politics: A

Critique of Some Pluralist and Structuralist Myths', *International Journal of Urban and Regional Research*, vol. 1, pp. 193–218.

Dunleavy, P. (1980) *Urban Political Analysis* (London: Macmillan).

Dunleavy, P. (1981) *The Politics of Mass Housing in Britain 1945–1975* (Oxford: Clarendon Press).

Dunning, J. (1979) 'The UK's International Investment Position in the Mid-1970s', *Lloyds Bank Review*, April, 132, pp. 1–21.

Eatwell, J. (1982) *Whatever Happened to Britain?* (London: Duckworth and BBC).

The Economist (1980) *Political Britain* (London: Economist Newspaper).

Elliot, J. M. (1981) *The Role of Law in Central–Local Relations* (London: Social Science Research Council).

Eltis, W. (1982) 'Do Government Manpower Cuts Correct Deficits When the Economy is in Deep Recession?', *Political Quarterly*, vol. 53, pp. 5–15.

Field, F., Meacher, M. and Pond, C. (1977) *To Him Who Hath: A Study of Poverty and Taxation* (Harmondsworth: Penguin).

Fothergill, S. and Gudgin, G. (1982) *Unequal Growth: Urban and Regional Employment Change in The UK* (London: Heinemann).

Friedman, A. (1977) *Industry and Labour* (London: Macmillan).

Friedman, M. (1977) 'From Galbraith to Economic Freedom', Occasional Paper 49, Institute of Economic Affairs.

Friend, A. and Metcalf, A. (1981) *Slump City* (London: Pluto Press).

Frost, M. and Spence, N. (1981) 'Policy Responses to Urban and Regional Economic Change in Britain', *Geographical Journal*, vol. 147, pp. 321–49.

Gamble, A. (1981) *Britain in Decline* (London: Macmillan).

Gibson, T. (1979) *People Power: Community and Work Groups in Action* (Harmondsworth: Penguin).

Glasgow University Media Group (GUMG) (1977) *Bad News* (London: Routledge & Kegan Paul).

Glasgow University Media Group (GUMG) (1980) *More Bad News* (London: Routledge & Kegan Paul).

Glyn, A. and Harrison, J. (1980) *The British Economic Disaster* (London: Pluto Press).

Glyn, A. and Sutcliffe, R. (1972) *British Capitalism, Workers and the Profit Squeeze* (Harmondsworth: Penguin).

Gough, I. (1979) *The Political Economy of The Welfare State* (London: Macmillan).

Greenwood, R. (1981) 'Fiscal Pressure and Local Government in England and Wales', in C. Hood and M. Wright (eds), *Big Government in Hard Times* (London: Martin Robertson).

Gregory, R. (1974) 'The Minister's Line: or the M4 Comes to Berkshire', in R. Kimber and J. J. Richardson (eds), *Campaigning for the Environment* (London: Routledge & Kegan Paul).

Griffith, J. A. G. (1974) 'Hailsham—Judge or Politician?', *New Statesman*, vol. 1, pp. 6–13.

Griffith, J. A. G. (1981, 2nd edn) *The Politics of The Judiciary* (London: Fontana).

Gurevitch, M., Woollacott, J., Bennett, T. and Curran, J. (1982) *Culture, Society and The Media* (London: Methuen).

Habermas, J. (1976) *Legitimation Crisis* (London: Heinemann).

Hain, P. (ed.) (1976) *Community Politics* (London: John Calder).

Hain, P. (ed.) (1979) *Policing the Police*, vol. 1 (London: John Calder).

Hall, J. M. (1982) *The Geography of Planning Decisions* (Oxford: Oxford University Press).

Hall, S. (1979) 'The great moving right show', *Marxism Today*, vol. 23, pp. 14–20.

Hall, S., Critcher, C., Jeffreson, T., Clarke, J. and Roberts, B. (1978) *Policing The Crisis: Mugging, The State and Law and Order* (London: Macmillan).

Hall, S. and Jacques, M. (eds) (1983) *The Politics of Thatcherism* (London: Lawrence & Wishart).

Hannah, L. (1976) *The Corporate Economy* (London: Methuen).

Hannah, L. and Kay, J. A. (1977) *Concentration in Modern Industry* (London: Macmillan).

Harloe, M. (1981) 'The Recommodification of Housing', in M. Harloe and E. Lepas (eds), *City, Class and Capital* (London: Edward Arnold).

Hartley, J. (1982) *Understanding News* (London: Methuen).

Harvey, D. (1982) *The Limits of Capital* (Oxford: Basil Blackwell).

Hayek, F. A. (1982) *Law, Legislation and Liberty* (London: Routledge & Kegan Paul).

Heclo, H. and Wildavsky, A. (1981, 2nd edn) *The Private Government of Public Money* (London: Macmillan).

Her Majesty's Inspectors (HMI) (1982) *Report on the Effects of Local Authority Expenditure Policies on the Education Service in England – 1981*.

Hindess, B. (1971) *The Decline of Working Class Politics* (London: MacGibbon & Kee).

Holland, S. (1975) *Strategy For Socialism* (London: Quartet).

Hood, C. (1981) 'Axeperson, Spare that Quango . . .', in C. Hood and M. Wright (eds), *Big Government in Hard Times* (Oxford: Martin Robertson).

Hood, C. and Wright, M. (eds) (1981) *Big Government in Hard Times* (Oxford: Martin Robertson).

Institute of Economic Affairs (IEA) (1979) *The Taming of Government*, IEA Readings 21.

Jessop, B. (1980) 'The Transformation of the State in Post-war Britain', in R. Scase (ed.), *The State in Western Europe* (London: Croom Helm).

Johnson, S. P. (1973) *The Politics of Environment* (London: Tom Stacey).

Jordan, B. (1982) *Mass Unemployment and The Future of Britain* (Oxford: Basil Blackwell).

Katznelson, I. (1981) *City Trenches* (New York: Pantheon).

Kaufman, G. (1982) 'Campaign Diary of a Local Government Bill Saboteur', *Guardian*, 12 July.

Kavanagh, D. (ed.) (1982) *The Politics of The Labour Party* (London: Allen & Unwin).

Keeble, D. (1976) *Industrial Location and Planning in The United Kingdom* (London: Methuen).

Keeble, D. (1978) 'Industrial Decline in the Inner City and Conurbation', *Transactions of the Institute of British Geographers* (New Series), vol. 3, pp. 101–14.

Kimber, R. and Richardson, J. (eds) (1974) *Campaigning For The Environment* (London: Routledge & Kegan Paul).

King, A. (1982) 'Whatever is Happening to the British Party System?', *Parliamentary Affairs*, vol. XXXV, pp. 241–51.

King, M. A. (1975) 'The UK Profit Crisis', *Economic Journal*, pp. 121–36.

Kirby, A. M. (1982) *The Politics of Location* (London: Methuen).

Kogan, M. (1978) *The Politics of Educational Change* (London: Fontana/Collins).

Labour Party (1981) *The Socialist Alternative* (London: Labour party).

Lawless, P. (1981) *Britain's Inner Cities: Problems and Policies* (London: Harper & Row).

Le Grand, J. (1982) *The Strategy of Inequality* (London: Allen & Unwin).

Leitch Committee (1977) *Report of the Advisory Committee on Trunk Road Assessment* (HMSO).

Lever, H. and Edwards, G. (1980a) 'Why Germany Beats Britain', *The Sunday Times*, 9 November.

Lever, H. and Edwards, G. (1980b) 'How to Bank on Britain', *The Sunday Times*, 16 November.

Mandel, E. (1978) *The Second Slump* (London: New Left Books).

Martin, R. L. (1982) 'Job Loss and Regional Incidence of Redundancies', *Cambridge Journal of Economics*, vol. 6, pp. 375–95.

Massey, D. (1982) 'City Crisis', *New Socialist*, vol. 4, pp. 38–41.

Massey, D. and Meegan, R. (1979) 'The Geography of Industrial Reorganisation', *Progress in Planning*, vol. 10, p. 3.

Massey, D. and Meegan, R. (1982) *The Anatomy of Job Loss* (London: Methuen).

Meadows, D. H., Meadows, D. L., Randers, J. and Behrens, III W. W. (1972) *The Limits To Growth* (New York: University Books).

Merseyside Socialist Research Group (1980) *Merseyside in Crisis* (Manchester: Manchester Free Press).

Middlemass, K. (1979) *Politics in Industrial Society: The Experience of the British System since 1911* (London: André Deutsch).

Midwinter, A. and Page, E. (1981) 'Cutting Local Spending – The Scottish Experience 1976–80', in Hood and Wright (eds), *Big Government in Hard Times*.

Miller, S. M. (1978) 'The Recapitalisation of Capitalism', *International Journal of Urban and Regional Research*, vol. 2, pp. 202–12.

Morgan, A. D. (1979) 'Foreign Manufacturing by UK Firms', in Blackaby (ed.), *Deindustrialisation*.

Munton, R. J. C. (1977) 'Financial Institutions: Their Ownership of Agricultural Land in Britain', *Area*, vol. 9, pp. 29–37.

Murgatroyd, L. (1981) 'Deindustrialisation in Lancaster', Working Paper, Lancaster Regionalism Group.

Murphy, D. (1976) *The Silent Watchdog* (London: Constable).

Newton, K. (1981) 'The Local Financial Crisis in Britain: A Non-Crisis Which is Neither Local nor Financial', in L. J. Sharpe (ed.), *The Local Fiscal Crisis in Western Europe* (London, Beverley Hills: Sage).

Northfield Report (1979) *Committee of Inquiry into the Acquisition and Occupancy of Agricultural Land*, Cmnd 7599 (London: HMSO).

North Tyneside Community Development Project (CDP) (1978) *North Shields: Living with Industrial Change* (London: CDP).

O'Connor, J. (1973) *The Fiscal Crisis of The State* (New York: St James).

O'Malley, J. (1977) *The Politics of Community Action* (Nottingham: Spokesman).

O'Riordan, T. (1980, 2nd edn) *Environmentalism* (London: Pion).

Owen, D. (1981) *Face The Future* (London: Jonathan Cape).

Philo, G., Hewitt, J., Beharrell, P. and Davis, H. (1982) *Really Bad News* (London: Writers & Readers).

Plender, J. (1982) *That's The Way The Money Goes: The Financial Institutions and The Nation's Savings* (London: André Deutsch).

Pliatzky, L. (1982a) *Getting and Spending* (Oxford: Basil Blackwell).

Pliatzky, L. (1982b) 'Cash Limits and Pay Policy', *Political Quarterly*, vol. 53, pp. 16–23.

Pollard, S. (1982) *The Wasting of The British Economy* (London: Croom Helm).

Pond, C. (1982) 'Taxation and Public Expenditure', in A. Walker (ed.), *Public Expenditure and Social Policy* (London: Heinemann).

Ravetz, A. (1980) *Remaking Cities* (London: Croom Helm).

Reiner, R. (1978) *The Blue-Coated Worker* (Cambridge: Cambridge University Press).

Rex, J. (1982) 'The 1981 Urban Riots in Britain', *International Journal of Urban and Regional Research*, vol. 6, pp. 99–113.

Ridley, N. (1978) *The Economist*, 27 May.

Rodgers, W. (1982) *The Politics of Change* (London: Secker & Warburg).

Rowbotham, S., Segal, L. and Wainwright, H. (1979) *Beyond The Fragments: Feminism and the Making of Socialism* (London: Merlin Press).

Sampson, A. (1982) *The Changing Anatomy of Britain* (London: Hodder & Stoughton).

Samuel, R. (1982) 'Tawney and the SDP', *Guardian*, 29 March and 5 April.

Sandbach, F. (1980) *Environment, Ideology and Policy* (Oxford: Basil Blackwell).

Sarlvik, B. and Crewe, I. (1983) *Decade of Dealignment?* (Cambridge: Cambridge University Press).

Saunders, P. (1979) *Urban Politics* (London: Hutchinson).

Saunders, P. (1980) 'Local Government and the State', *New Society*, pp. 550–1.

Saunders, P. (1981) *Social Theory and The Urban Question* (London: Hutchinson).

Scarman Report (1981) *The Brixton Disorders April 10–12th 1981*, Cmnd 8427 (London: HMSO).

Seabrook, J. (1982) Agenda article, *Guardian*, 1 March.

Short, J. R. (1982a) *An Introduction to Political Geography* (London: Routledge & Kegan Paul).

Short, J. R. (1982b) *Housing in Britain: The Post-War Experience* (London: Methuen).

Short, J. R. (1982c) 'Urban Policy and British Cities', *Journal of the American Planning Association*, Winter, pp. 39–52.

Short, J. R. and Bassett, K. A. (1981) 'Housing Policy and the Inner City in the 1970s', *Transactions of the Institute of British Geographers, New Series*, vol. 6, pp. 293–312.

Smith, L. and Jones, D. (eds) (1981) *Deprivation, Participation and Community Action* (London: Routledge & Kegan Paul).

Starkie, D. (1982) *The Motorway Age: Road and Traffic Policies in Post-War Britain* (Oxford: Pergamon).

Stephenson, H. (1982) *Claret and Chips: The Rise of The SDP* (London: Michael Joseph).

Stewart, M. (1978) *Politics and Economic Policy in the UK Since 1964* (Oxford: Pergamon).

Taylor, P. J. (1979) 'The Changing Geography of Representation in Britain', *Area*, vol. 11, pp. 289–94.

Taylor, R. (1980) *The Fifth Estate: Britain's Unions in The Modern World* (London: Pan).

Thompson, E. P. (1980) *Writing By Candlelight* (London: Merlin Press).

Thurow, L. (1981) *The Zero-sum Society* (Penguin: Harmondsworth).

Treasury (1977) *Public Expenditure to 1980/81*, Cmnd 6721 (London: HMSO).

Treasury (1979) *The Government's Expenditure Plan 1979/80 to 1982/83*, Cmnd 7439 (London: HMSO).

Treasury (1980) *The Government's Expenditure Plans 1980/81 to 1983/84*. Cmnd 7841 (London: HMSO).

Treasury (1981a) 'Ending Exchange Controls', *Economic Progress Report*, No. 138.

Treasury (1981b) 'The Impact of the Recession on the PSBR', *Economic Progress Report*, No. 130.

Treasury (1982) *The Government's Expenditure Plans 1982–83 to 1984–85*, Cmnd 8494 (London: HMSO).

Tulloch, J. (1982) *The Development of The British Mass Media 1880–1980* (London: Methuen).

Walker, A. (ed.) (1982) *Public Expenditure and Social Policy* (London: Heinemann).

Ward, M. (1982) 'Local Economic Development: The Local Authority Role', Lecture delivered to the Human Geography and Planning Colloquia, University of Reading, 9 November.

Wates, N. (1976) *The Battle for Tolmers Square* (London: Routledge & Kegan Paul).

Whale, J. (1977) *The Politics of the Media* (London: Fontana/Collins).

194   *Bibliography*

Wilson Report (1980) *Committee to Review the Functioning of Financial Institutions*, Cmnd 7939 (London: HMSO).

Wright, M. (ed.) (1980) *Public Spending Decisions* (London: Allen & Unwin).

Wright, M. (1981) 'Big Government in Hard Times: The Restraint of Public Expenditure', in Hood and Wright (eds), *Big Government in Hard Times*.

Index

202 *Index*

Thompson, E. P – *continued*
  on trend towards authoritarianism in
    Britain 115–16
Times, The 116
Tolmers Square, Camden: residents stop
    commercial development of 147
Town and Country Planning Acts
  of 1947 168
  of 1968 167
trade unions
  capital's moves to control 44–5
  public sector employees and fiscal
    crisis 96–101: classification of
    unions by power 99; Conservative
    government's line 98–9; govern-
    ment adoption of cash limits
    policy 97–8; theories on need to
    reduce public sector 97–8, 101;
    union failures and successes 100;
    union membership 97; union–
    government clashes 97, 99
  resistance to redundancy 37
  strength in public sector 99
  weakened by unemployment 42, 49
Trade Unions and Labour Relations Act
    1974 45
Trade Union Congress (TUC) 65
Treasury 28, 34, 66
  on financial effects of slump 85–6
  White Paper on restraining public
    expenditure 82
Trident missile programme 16

unemployment 13, 19, 22, 36–7
  lack of investment and 54, 62
  media coverage of 121–2
  regional variations 39, 40, 41–2,
    62–3
  youthful 37, 40–1, 62

United States: beneficiary of post-war
    boom 9
University Grants Committee 101
Upper Clyde Shipbuilders 30, 37
  union resistance to closure 1972 37
Urban Aid Programme 91
Urban Development Corporations 70
urbanisation
  becomes the norm 1
  capital in urban arena 3–4
  community, the, in urban arena 4–5
  focus of the present book 2
  inner city poverty 1
  nineteenth century 1
  state, the, in urban arena 5–7

Walker, A. 82
Wates, N.: on Tolmers Square victory
    over commercial developers 47
welfare state
  benefits and beneficiaries 81
  expenditure on 77, 79
  inflation and 79
  welfare expectations 79
West Midlands
  decline of manufacturing 39
  unemployment 39–41
Whale, John 120
  on symbiotic relation between govern-
    ment and media 117
White Paper of 1944 9
Whitelaw, William 114
Wilson, Harold 54
  1980 committee's review of financial
    institutions 54
Winchester: success of M3 Joint Action
    Group (JAG) 149
Wright, M.: on attempts to restrain
    public expenditure 83